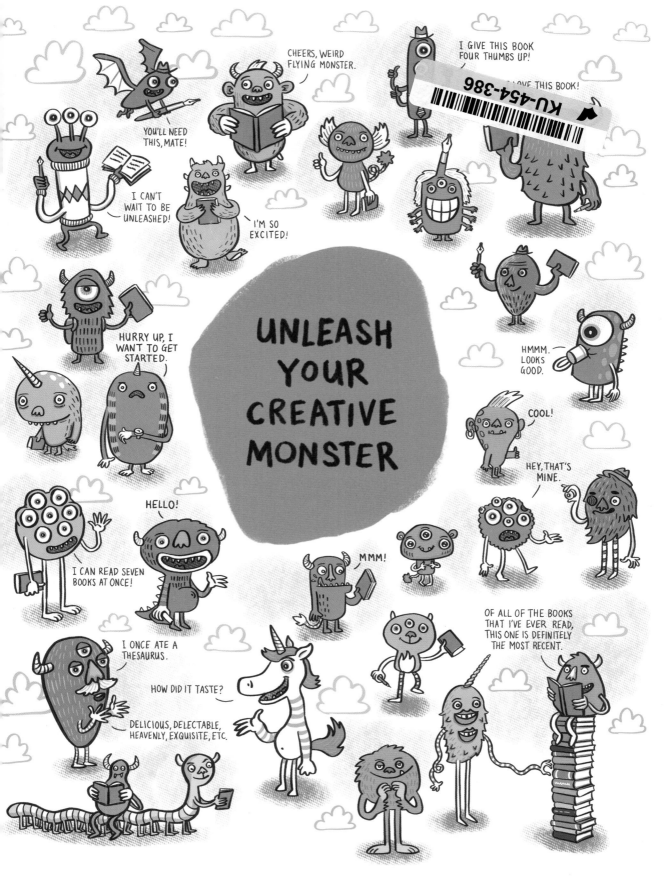

UNLEASH YOUR CREATIVE MONSTER

A CHILDREN'S GUIDE TO WRITING

ANDY JONES (WITH A LITTLE HELP FROM RUBY & EVIE)

ILLUSTRATIONS BY *Olaf Falafel*

FOR RUBY AND EVIE,
YOU'RE ROARSOME XXX — A.J.

FOR ROBBIE AND WILLIAM,
MY TWO FAVOURITE MONSTERS — O.F.

FIRST PUBLISHED 2021 BY WALKER BOOKS LTD, 87 VAUXHALL WALK, LONDON SE11 5HJ

2 4 6 8 10 9 7 5 3 1

TEXT © 2021 ANDY JONES • ILLUSTRATIONS © 2021 OLAF FALAFEL

THE RIGHT OF ANDY JONES TO BE IDENTIFIED AS AUTHOR AND OLAF FALAFEL TO BE IDENTIFIED AS ILLUSTRATOR RESPECTIVELY
OF THIS WORK HAS BEEN ASSERTED BY THEM IN ACCORDANCE WITH THE COPYRIGHT, DESIGNS AND PATENTS ACT 1988

THIS BOOK HAS BEEN TYPESET IN STEMPEL SCHNEIDLER, CHALKDUSTER, LIQUID EMBRACE AND HALEWYN

PRINTED IN CHINA

BRITISH LIBRARY CATALOGUING IN PUBLICATION DATA: A CATALOGUE RECORD FOR THIS BOOK IS AVAILABLE FROM THE BRITISH LIBRARY

ISBN 978-1-4063-9662-1

WWW.WALKER.CO.UK

CONTENTS

I MAY LOOK LIKE AN ORDINARY SNAIL, BUT I'M ALSO A MUSE.

FIND OUT ABOUT MUSES, MONSTERS AND WHAT MAKES A GREAT STORY IN THE NEXT FEW PAGES.

SECTION ONE: TRAINING YOUR CREATIVE MONSTER

LEVEL 1: STORY BASICS

LEVEL 2: ESSENTIAL SKILLS FOR STORYTELLERS

IN THIS SECTION I'LL SHOW YOU ALL 72 OF MY CHARACTER TRAITS.

AND WE VISIT FROM THE PLANET BLAH TO TALK ABOUT TENSES.

LET'S GO, SUSAN!

LEVEL 3: SECRET WEAPONS OF THE WORDSMITH

WE'LL BE TALKING ABOUT PISTOLS, POTIONS, PONGS AND THE POWER OF DETAILS.

SECTION TWO: MONSTER MISTAKES

IN THIS SECTION, THEY'RE FIRING ME OUT OF A CANNON.

IT MIGHT SOUND LIKE A MISTAKE, BUT I PROMISE IT'LL BE GOOD.

IF YOU'RE A FAN OF WEIRD STUFF YOU'LL ENJOY MY BIT ON PAGE 123.

SECTION THREE: WHEN YOUR MONSTER GETS STUCK

CREATIVE MONSTERS NEED A NUTRITIOUS AND VARIED DIET. THAT'S WHAT THE NEXT SECTION IS ALL ABOUT.

SECTION FOUR: FEEDING YOUR CREATIVE MONSTER

FIRST, LET'S MEET **ANDY**
WHO WROTE THIS BOOK

THE IDEA FOR THIS BOOK
CAME ON A RAINY DAY TWO SUMMERS AGO.

MY DAUGHTERS WERE LOOKING FOR SOMETHING INTERESTING
TO DO THAT DIDN'T INVOLVE GETTING WET. WELL, I WRITE NOVELS FOR A
JOB, SO I GAVE MY GIRLS A STORY PROMPT AND CHALLENGED THEM TO WRITE
A STORY IN 30 MINUTES. AND THEY DID. IN FACT, THEY ENJOYED IT SO MUCH
THEY ASKED FOR ANOTHER. I GAVE THEM ANOTHER, AND THEY WROTE THAT ONE
TOO. BY THE TIME THEY ASKED FOR A THIRD PROMPT (VERY DEMANDING, MY
DAUGHTERS), THE IDEA FOR *UNLEASH YOUR CREATIVE MONSTER* HAD FORMED.

AND NOW YOU ARE HOLDING THAT BOOK IN YOUR HANDS.
I HOPE IT INSPIRES YOU AS MUCH AS MY
TWO MONSTERS INSPIRED ME.

AND OLAF WHO DREW THE PICTURES

HI! I'M OLAF AND I'M AN AUTHOR, AN ILLUSTRATOR, A DAD AND A STAND-UP COMEDIAN, WHICH IS EXACTLY THE SAME AS A STAND-UP CHAMELEON (EXCEPT I DON'T CHANGE COLOUR TO BLEND IN WITH MY BACKGROUND).

AS WELL AS TRYING TO MAKE PEOPLE LAUGH, I DRAW A LOT. IN FACT, I HAVE ILLUSTRATED ALL OF THE MONSTERS IN THIS BOOK AND HAVE ALSO WRITTEN THE FUNNY THINGS THAT COME OUT OF THEIR MOUTHS (AND SOMETIMES THEIR BUMS).

I HOPE YOU ENJOY THIS BOOK. LET ME KNOW WHICH MONSTERS YOU LIKE BEST — I THINK THE DRAWINGS ON PAGE 165 ARE MY FAVOURITE!

SO WHAT'S ALL THIS ABOUT A CREATIVE MONSTER?

If you ask me, writing is the most fun you can have outside of a trampoline. But I know what you're thinking: *when grown-ups say something is fun, it usually isn't!* So, don't take my word for it, let's ask my daughters, Ruby and Evie.

See, I told you it was fun. And this book, I promise, will be fun too. It contains lots of tips and ideas to inspire you, build your writing muscles and unleash your Creative Monster.

"Whoa whoa whoa!" I hear you cry. "Did you say 'Monster'? Tell me more about this *monster*."

To which I say: Sure thing. But first, let me tell you about "The Muse". In ancient Greece, there were nine goddesses known as the Muses – they were said to inspire artists, writers and thinkers to produce original and dazzling work. Even now, thousands of years later, writers and artists talk about their "muse" – the mysterious force that brings bright ideas into being. Some people call this force "inspiration". Others call it our "genius". I call mine the "Creative Monster".

Why a monster?

I'm glad you asked. Monsters are exciting, unpredictable, powerful. They can be scary at times, but, if handled with love, surprisingly tender. They are often made of unusual parts from different places, and this is what makes them magnificent, fascinating and irresistible.

12

So, yeah, my muse is a monster. If that's all right by you? And guess what? You have a Creative Monster too. Every single one of us does. It may be that your Creative Monster is sleeping at the moment, or small and timorous,* but don't worry, we're going to wake your monster, feed it, exercise it and watch it grow into the big, beautiful, crazy, rampaging creature it is destined to become.

MY MONSTER IS MADE OF JELLY AND COVERED IN LETTERS. IT HAS A BIG BLUE TONGUE TO SLURP UP ALL THE INFORMATION FROM THE BOOKS I READ. WHEN I GET STUCK, MY MONSTER WILL GIVE ME A BIG CUDDLE AND CALM ME DOWN WHILST RESTORING THE INFORMATION IT GOBBLED UP BACK INTO MY BRAIN.

MY CREATIVE MONSTER LOOKS LIKE A PENGUIN AND HAS SEVERAL SPECIAL ABILITIES. IF I GET STUCK, IT WHISPERS AN IDEA FROM ITS BEAK STRAIGHT INTO MY BRAIN SO I GET UNSTUCK. ALSO, WHENEVER SHE WANTS, MY PENGUIN CAN CHANGE COLOUR, EVEN INTO COMBINATIONS THAT DON'T GO VERY WELL TOGETHER.

MONSTERS NEED LAIRS

Traditionally, monsters live in caves, swamps, under bridges – you know the kinds of places. But Creative Monsters live on paper. If you can, I'd like you to find a notebook to use alongside this book. We're going to fill your notebook with fun exercises and exciting stories – we're going to make it a lair for your Creative Monster.

If you don't have a notebook, a pile of loose pages in a carrier bag will make a perfectly good lair. Perhaps your lair is a file on a computer – whatever suits you and your monster. This lair is a place where you can have fun, take chances, make big discoveries and big mistakes. It's a place of freedom and adventure.

When you have a special place for your writing, your writing becomes more special to you. So, before we go any further, go and find somewhere for your Creative Monster to live. If you do use a book, you can decorate the cover in a style that will make your monster comfortable.

EXERCISE
MEET YOUR CREATIVE MONSTER

Now that you have a home for your Creative Monster,
write a few lines to explain what your monster looks like
and how it will help you with your writing. If you like, you can
draw your monster before you describe it. Think about:

- Size and shape
- Smells and noises
- Paws, claws and tentacles
- Fur, hair and scales

You don't need to include all these details,
they are simply there to inspire you.

One more thing: your Creative Monster needs a name,
but whatever you do, don't tell anyone what it is.
This is important, because that mystery – that secret
bond between writer and monster – is part of its power.

When you've finished, come and meet
me in the section called "Training
Your Creative Monster".

LEVEL 1
STORY BASICS

We're ready to begin your training, to hone
your skills and get your Creative Monster roaring.
Your training will be divided into three sections,
each focusing on a different aspect of your writing.

First we will cover the basic elements of a
great story. We'll learn what makes a narrative
move forward and – importantly – what keeps
your readers reading.

And we're going to write some stories of our
own, so grab your pencil, take your Creative
Monster by the paw (or flipper, or
whatever) and follow me.

A GREAT STORY IS LIKE A GOOD CAKE
THE IMPORTANCE OF GOALS, PROBLEMS AND STRUGGLES

Before we talk about stories, let's talk about cake. What is a cake? Is it the icing, the chocolate buttons, the candles? No. These things exist to make a cake more interesting, more tempting, more delicious. But without a cake to hold them all together, what you have is a bit of a mess.

Stories are the same. We enjoy clever descriptions, exciting battles, funny moments and interesting characters – but these things work best when they are supported by a great cake. Sorry, I mean a great story.

Stories have three main ingredients – **Goals**, **Problems** and **Struggles**. And if you take only one thing from this book, make it the importance of Goals, Problems and Struggles. Everything else – like the icing on a cake – is just an added bonus.

EVERYTHING ELSE

STRUGGLES

PROBLEMS

GOALS

A TASTY STORY

MY GOAL IS TO EAT THIS CAKE.

SALIVATING MONSTER

Let's look at an example.

Suppose we have a woman walking up a mountain. Is that a story? Well, she has a **goal** – to reach the top of the mountain – but unless we give her a problem, all we have is a woman going for a walk. And that is not a story – people do that every day.

ARE WE THERE YET?

THIS IS OK, BUT IT COULD BE A TAD MORE EXCITING.

What if she gets lost? Say a gust of wind rips the map from her hands and sends it swirling into a river below – now we have something. We have a **problem**. And we have a question – "what happens next?" Will our hero give up and go home? Or will she **struggle** to achieve her goal? She'll struggle of course, because that makes for a much better story. Perhaps she dives into the river after her map, or maybe she climbs a tree to get a better view of the mountain. But she doesn't give up; she solves the problem, and she continues on her way.

I'M A PROBLEM!

(ACTUALLY I'M QUITE NICE REALLY, I'M JUST PRETENDING TO BE SCARY TO MAKE THE STORY MORE INTERESTING.)

But now we – as writers of this story – have a problem of our own. As soon as our hero finds the path, the story loses energy. It's just a woman walking up a big hill again. So, we give her another problem to solve:

How about a snowstorm?

An earthquake?

A rampaging bear?

All bad for our hero, but all great for our story. Eventually, of course, we let our **heroes*** achieve their goals. Or fail, if we think it makes a better ending. But not until we have pushed them over, tripped them up, tied them down and made them struggle more than they have ever struggled before. Because the tougher the struggle, the more satisfying the story. Sounds cruel, I know. But that's a story. And besides, it's so much fun.

Story problems, by the way, don't have to be as dramatic as a snowstorm up a mountain. They can be small things or funny things. Sometimes, they exist only inside the character's head. For example: a boy wants to enter an art competition with a big prize. But although he's talented, he lacks the confidence to enter. He's afraid he will be disappointed or, worse, humiliated if he doesn't win. Here, the hero's struggle is against *himself*.

OK, I think we're ready to write our first story.

*When you hear the word HERO, you probably think of a character that performs acts of extreme courage: a knight, a spy, a champion of some sort. But in the world of stories, hero simply means the main character. Your hero doesn't have to be brave; they don't have to know kung fu. A hero can be shy, quiet, thoughtful or fearful – in fact, these types of "heroes" make very interesting characters.

READY, STEADY, STORY!
THE ART OF WRITING FEARLESSLY

We're about to tackle our first story prompt, and I would recommend that you tackle it quickly. Ideally, I would like you to write it in one go, working for somewhere between 20 minutes and an hour.

The great thing about writing stories to a time limit is, to put it simply: it stops you messing about and being distracted. Without a time limit, we might spend too much time deciding where to start, what the character is called and what colour his socks are. All of which is fine, but too much pondering can slow you down. It can stop you in your tracks.

There's no time for that when the clock is ticking. You spend a few minutes (no more than five) thinking about what you're going to write and then you go for it. You write as fast and fearlessly as you can. No stopping. No going back. Something doesn't feel right? Keep going. Can't think of a name for your character? Call him, or her, Billy. Can't remember a fact? Make it up. Keep writing and keep moving forwards.

Will it be perfect? Of course not, but there will be plenty of time to fix it later – to change the beginning, expand the middle, adjust the end. For now… *Just. Keep. Writing.*

WONKY STORIES, MIX-UPS AND MISTAKES ARE NOTHING TO WORRY ABOUT. IN FACT, THEY ARE A GREAT WAY TO LEARN AND IMPROVE YOUR WRITING. WE'LL TALK MORE ABOUT THIS IN THE SECTION CALLED "MONSTER MISTAKES".

CAN I HAVE MY BOOK BACK, PLEASE? I NEED TO FINISH EATING, ERR, I MEAN, WRITING.

To begin with, why not set a time limit of around 30 minutes and see how that works for you? But remember, this is your book and you should use it however you want. If you are happier spending extra time thinking about your story before you start, then do so. If you want to write for longer than 30 minutes, or if your story (because stories are living things) wants you to keep on going, then keep on going! If you want to change the prompt, a little or a lot, well, that's fine too. The important thing is simply to write.

So, let's get our notebooks and write something, shall we?

THAT'S IT. TIME'S UP!

CONGRATULATIONS! IT DOESN'T MATTER IF YOUR STORIES AREN'T PERFECT.

MINE TASTED PERFECT.

OOOH, I LIKE THIS QUOTE.

"WE LEARN FROM FAILURE, NOT SUCCESS."
BRAM STOKER, AUTHOR OF *DRACULA*

(I READ THIS WHEN I WAS 14, AND IT IS STILL ONE OF THE SCARIEST BOOKS I HAVE EVER READ.)

WOO HOO!

THE SPIDER WHOSE WEB WOULDN'T SPIN

Talk about embarrassing, right? All the other spiders are spinning beautiful webs, but one spider – Tiny Jack – just can't do it. Before you start writing, let's look at this story prompt in terms of goals, problems and struggles.

Goals: At first glance, Tiny Jack's goal is to spin a web. But can we make this more specific (and, therefore, more interesting)? Why does Tiny Jack want to spin a web?

Problems: He can't spin webs. But, again, why?

Struggles: How will Tiny Jack overcome his problem to achieve his goal?

Enough from me, it's time to spin a story.
Aim for 30 minutes of writing,
but if your story is flowing,
keep on going.

SPIDERS SPIN WEBS TO CATCH FOOD:
IN OTHER WORDS, FLIES.

BUT WHAT WOULD THIS MEAN FOR A SPIDER WHOSE WEB WON'T SPIN?

MAYBE THERE'S ANOTHER REASON SPINNING WEBS IS IMPORTANT TO TINY JACK? SOMETHING LIKE ... A WEB-SPINNING CONTEST?

NOW WHAT ABOUT THIS "WEB PROBLEM"?

IS IT DOWN TO A LACK OF CONFIDENCE?

OR SOMETHING PHYSICAL?

OR MAYBE TINY JACK ISN'T A SPIDER AFTER ALL...

AVALANCHE!
AN INTRODUCTION TO PLOT

When people talk about stories, they often talk about "plot". You can think of the plot as a collective noun for all the important events that happen in your story.

And these events – these *important* events – are called **plot points**: the surprises, fights, kisses, explosions, chases, deals, betrayals, discoveries, arguments and so on.

EXPLOSIONS

DISCOVERIES

SURPRISES

BOOM!

CHASES

KISSES

FIGHTS

Plots can be complex, twisty and dramatic, or simple, straightforward and subtle. But good plots have one thing in common – the "plot points" are all connected.

I CAN SEE NO POSSIBLE SCENARIO IN WHICH THIS ENDS BADLY.

I TAKE THAT BACK!

You know how when you roll a snowball down a hill, it gathers more snow and grows beneath your gloved hands until it is huge and heavy and spectacular? Well, good plots are the same. We start with one simple thing, then we push it, we add to it and we make it grow.

Let's go back to our luckless mountaineer and see what connected plot points look like:

WHAT CAN YOU SEE?

I'M NOT SURE, BUT IT LOOKS A BIT LIKE A GOOD PLOT.

Joan was climbing a mountain when she dropped her map ⟶ So she climbed a tree to get a better view, but she slipped on an icy branch and fell, twisting her ankle ⟶ She screamed for help, but the sound of her voice started an avalanche ⟶ Joan crawled into the safety of a cave and hid as the snow tumbled past ⟶ However, it became apparent this cave was occupied. She heard a low snarling sound, she saw a pair of yellow eyes in the darkness...*

*Note, this still isn't a story; it's simply a list of plot points. Each point will need writing out, complete with descriptions, feelings, details and more. Some plot points might consist of a single sentence, others might take several paragraphs.

Plot points that aren't connected read like this:

Joan was climbing a mountain when she dropped her map ⟶
She continued climbing but there was an avalanche ⟶
She escaped the avalanche, kept walking and then
bumped into a yeti.

Disconnected plot points feel random and confusing. No matter how interesting each event is, they don't stick together as a story. At best you are left with a collection of nice, but small, snowballs. On the other hand, connected plot points pile up on top of each other, forming a gigantic snowball of obstacles, struggles, big events and dramatic consequences. Who knows, if you push it hard enough, you might even create an avalanche!

WHY IS THE PLOT ALWAYS SO DANGEROUS?

I NEVER SIGNED UP FOR THIS!

SHUT UP AND RUN!

CATS, MATS AND ROBBING BANKS
THE IMPORTANCE OF CONFLICT

A famous writer called John le Carré has a great way of describing stories. He said: "'The cat sat on the mat' is not the beginning of a story, but 'the cat sat on the dog's mat' is."

Mr Le Carré is describing **conflict** – a big disagreement, argument or battle between characters. And it's a great way of creating problems and struggles for your story. Conflict can be as small as a squabble between pets over a mat, or as large as two countries going to war. Here are some examples of conflict:

Mike wants to rob a bank, but his friend Andy (the sensible one!) thinks it's a bad idea.

Suzi wants to go to the cinema; Karolina wants to go for pizza.

Two squirrels spot the same delicious nut.

I SAW IT FIRST!

FOR THE LAST TIME, MOTHER, I REFUSE TO EAT THIS TASTELESS SLOP.

A mummy is trying to feed porridge to a baby. But the baby refuses the food.

The size or silliness of the conflict doesn't matter. What matters is that both sides believe they are right. Tempers are lost, voices are raised, friendships are tested and things get ugly! And no one likes it when things get ugly. Well, except for writers. We love it!

Conflict is a powerful force in stories. It creates tension – the feeling of two forces pulling in opposite directions – which, in turn, creates drama. Conflict can also create uncertainty – will Mike rob the bank? Will the characters ever be friends again? All of these things give your story energy and keep your readers reading – which is rather important in a story, wouldn't you say?

WHO ARE YOU CALLING UGLY?

31

THE CAT SAT ON THE DOG'S MAT

It's time to grab your notebook, a pen and your Creative Monster. Find somewhere where you won't be disturbed for the next 30 minutes, make yourself comfortable and write a story involving a cat, a dog and a snuggly (if a bit stinky) mat.

Ready? Go.

DOCTOR FRANKENSTEIN HAD IT RIGHT
GENRES: WHAT THEY ARE AND HOW TO MIX THEM

Do you know the story of Frankenstein?* The mad scientist who made a monster by stitching together bits from a whole bunch of different bodies? Scary stuff, for sure, and a wonderful story. But also a great example of how we can combine separate elements to create something awesome.

BWA HA HA!
MY MOST HIDEOUS CREATION TO DATE IS ALMOST COMPLETE. I SHALL CALL HIM ...

... COLIN!

*FRANKENSTEIN was written by Mary Shelley after she and two friends (both famous poets) decided to see who could write the scariest story. It's safe to assume Mary won, and 200 years later her story is still scaring the living daylights out of new readers. This is a great example of what can happen when we set ourselves a writing challenge.

A QUICK GUIDE TO GENRES

A **genre** is a style of story. Here's a list of *some* of the most popular story genres and some of the elements they contain:

ACTION IS MY MIDDLE NAME! (NOT REALLY, IT'S RAYMOND.)

ACTION
(CHASES, FIGHTS, EXPLOSIONS)

THE REALLY SCARY PART ...

... IS HOW SLEEPING IN A COFFIN MESSES UP YOUR HORNS.

HORROR
(MONSTERS, MANIACS, MAD SCIENTISTS)

I NEED YOU TO TAKE THIS RING ACROSS THE LAKE OF FIRE, THROUGH THE HAUNTED FOREST AND BACK TO THE SHOP WHERE I BOUGHT IT.

THE RECEIPT'S IN THE BAG.

FANTASY
(WITCHES, FAIRIES, MAGIC)

YOU'RE THE ONLY ONE FOR ME.

ROMANCE
(LOVE, KISSING, MISUNDERSTANDINGS)

AT LAST, THE GOLDEN BANANA IS MINE!

ADVENTURE
(MAPS, SHIPS, JUNGLES, TREASURE)

SCIENCE FICTION
(ALIENS, TIME TRAVEL, WEIRD GIZMOS)

HISTORY
(VICTORIANS, EGYPTIANS, THE WORLD WARS)

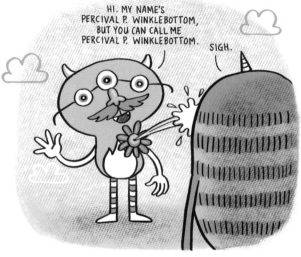

COMEDY
(SLIP-UPS, MIX-UPS, CRAZY CHARACTERS, STICKY SITUATIONS)

WESTERNS
(COWBOYS, GUNFIGHTS, GOLD)

MYSTERY
(DETECTIVES, MURDERS, CLUES)

Think about your favourite stories and see if you can decide which genre they fit into. And what elements they contain. It can be tricky, because the best stories combine elements from different genres. The way Doctor Frankenstein combined parts of different bodies (yuck!).

You and your own Creative Monster can do this too. Write a funny mystery story, or a romance set in a haunted house, or an action story set in Victorian England. Break the genre rules, chop them up and stitch them back together into your own wonderful (or horrifying) creation.

LET'S MAKE A MASH-UP

A mash-up is when we take two or more things that don't normally sit together and then mix them. We mash 'em up.

One of my favourite examples is a film for grown-ups called *Shaun of the Dead*. (You can watch it when you're eighteen. And not before!) It's a zombie film mashed up with romance and comedy. I suppose you could call it a zom-rom-com. And it's great.

So go back to the list of genres on the previous page, and see if you can come up with some interesting mash-ups of your own. And if you find a good one, go ahead and write it.

THINK ABOUT THE TYPES OF CHARACTERS THAT GO WITH EACH GENRE.

CHARACTERS LIKE: HERO, EVIL GENIUS, EXPLORER, PIRATE, SHY PERSON, VAMPIRE, WEREWOLF, KING, PRINCESS, KNIGHT, TROLL, WIZARD, ALIEN, ROBOT, PILOT, OLD LADY, VICAR, NAUGHTY CHILDREN, SOLDIER, SPY, THIEF, DETECTIVE.

THEN THROW TWO UNLIKELY CHARACTERS TOGETHER AND THINK OF ALL THE FUNNY, SCARY, DRAMATIC AND EXCITING SCENES THAT MIGHT HAPPEN BETWEEN THEM.

HERO   EVIL GENIUS   WIZARD   SQUIRREL

LEVEL 2
ESSENTIAL SKILLS FOR STORYTELLERS

I LOVED LEVEL 1, CAKE _AND_ PORRIDGE!

I'VE HEARD THERE'S EVEN MORE PORRIDGE ON THE SIMILES PAGE.

WOO HOO!

Congratulations on completing Level 1 of your training. Or, if you jumped straight to this page, welcome to Level 2 of training your Creative Monster.

In Level 1, we looked at the elements that make a great story: obstacles, goals, struggle and conflict. And we discussed plot, genre and Doctor Frankenstein.

Next, we're going to look at some ideas and tools that will bring your writing to life – ways of making **characters** real, **descriptions** vivid, **dialogue** interesting and more!

Are you ready for Level 2?
Good. Let's get to it…

BUILDING HUMANS
(AND OTHER CREATURES)
HOW TO CREATE REALISTIC CHARACTERS

Interesting characters – just like interesting people – are defined by more than one thing. More than good or bad, brave or afraid, silly or smart. Interesting characters tend to be more complicated, with several sides – or traits* – to their personality.

A character who is relentlessly bad is fine, for a while, but they can become a bit predictable. A bit boring. But if this thoroughly horrible character is afraid of his mother, or all lovey-dovey with his cat, then we have seen another side to him, and he becomes more realistic and more interesting to the reader.

Or a girl who is shy at school, shy at home, shy at parties but fearless and terrifying when she practises judo. As a writer, you can work with that. You can use it to build a story.

When building a character, the different aspects of their personality don't have to be opposites like shy and fearless. They simply need to be varied and interesting.

> DON'T OVERDO IT! ONE MAJOR TRAIT, AND ONE OR TWO SUPPORTING TRAITS, ARE PLENTY FOR THE AVERAGE SHORT STORY. MORE THAN THIS AND YOUR CHARACTER WILL BE JUMBLED AND HARD TO GET TO KNOW. CONFUSING FOR YOU, YOUR CHARACTER AND YOUR READER.

*For the purpose of writing a story, a TRAIT is part of a character's personality – a thing that they do, or a way they behave. You'll find a huge list of character traits on the next page.

A WHOLE LOAD OF CHARACTER TRAITS

This list is just the beginning; there are hundreds and thousands of possible character traits. Almost as many as there are people in the world! See if you can think of some of your own and write them down in your notebook.

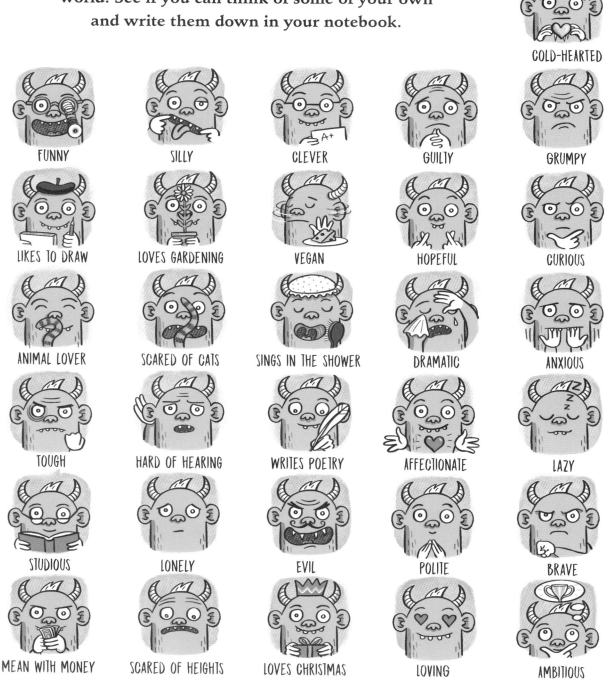

HOT-HEADED

COLD-HEARTED

FUNNY

SILLY

CLEVER

GUILTY

GRUMPY

LIKES TO DRAW

LOVES GARDENING

VEGAN

HOPEFUL

CURIOUS

ANIMAL LOVER

SCARED OF CATS

SINGS IN THE SHOWER

DRAMATIC

ANXIOUS

TOUGH

HARD OF HEARING

WRITES POETRY

AFFECTIONATE

LAZY

STUDIOUS

LONELY

EVIL

POLITE

BRAVE

MEAN WITH MONEY

SCARED OF HEIGHTS

LOVES CHRISTMAS

LOVING

AMBITIOUS

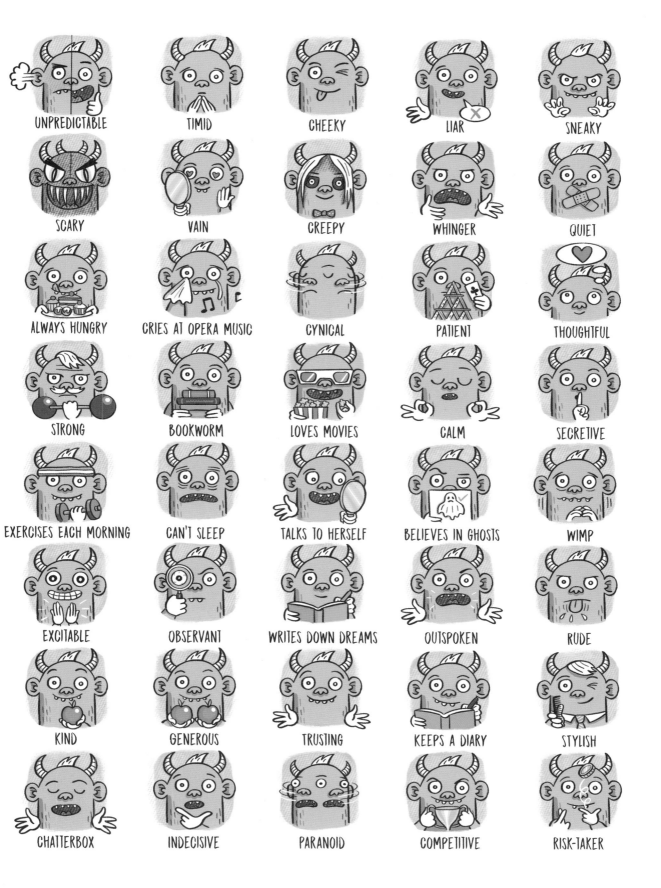

UNPREDICTABLE

TIMID

CHEEKY

LIAR

SNEAKY

SCARY

VAIN

CREEPY

WHINGER

QUIET

ALWAYS HUNGRY

CRIES AT OPERA MUSIC

CYNICAL

PATIENT

THOUGHTFUL

STRONG

BOOKWORM

LOVES MOVIES

CALM

SECRETIVE

EXERCISES EACH MORNING

CAN'T SLEEP

TALKS TO HERSELF

BELIEVES IN GHOSTS

WIMP

EXCITABLE

OBSERVANT

WRITES DOWN DREAMS

OUTSPOKEN

RUDE

KIND

GENEROUS

TRUSTING

KEEPS A DIARY

STYLISH

CHATTERBOX

INDECISIVE

PARANOID

COMPETITIVE

RISK-TAKER

EXERCISE
A CHARACTER IN CONFLICT

Imagine a character finding a £20 note lying on the pavement outside a church? Sounds like the start of a story, doesn't it?

What will your character do with the money?
Well, that will depend on the type of person they are.
If the character is defined by a single trait – charitable or mean – then the decision will be easy. And obvious.

But if your character has different personality traits – as most of us do, then their decision will be more difficult. Let's take the example of an honest character who loves football and needs a new ball. If that character finds £20, he will be in conflict with himself and you will have an interesting scene.

So let's build that character. Give him two or three personality traits, and then write a page or two showing what happens when he finds that money.

ARE THEY HONEST, CUNNING, MEAN, GENEROUS?

DO THEY NEED MONEY?

WHAT MIGHT THEY DO WITH IT IF THEY KEPT IT?

HOW OLD ARE THEY?

WHERE ARE THEY GOING?

WHERE HAVE THEY BEEN?

SHOW DON'T TELL
BUILDING EMOTION INTO YOUR WRITING

This is perhaps the best-known principle (an idea or rule) for writing fiction. When used properly, it can greatly improve the quality of your writing, helping your readers become involved in your story – experiencing it rather than simply reading it. Let me tell you what I mean. Better still, why don't I show you?

It was Sophia's first day in her new school and she was nervous.

Fine. This tells us something about Sophia. But does it make you feel anything? Do you share Sophia's nervousness? No? Well, I don't blame you. I blame me, because I haven't done anything other than tell you the facts in an unemotional way. Let's see if I can do better. Let's see if I can show you how Sophia is feeling by writing a short scene filled with revealing details. And the cool thing is, I don't even have to use the word "nervous".

Sophia checked her reflection one last time. She looked fine, no jam on her face, no toothpaste on her school uniform. Her hair was tied in a ponytail, but looking at it now, she wondered if it made her look a bit … swotty. What if the other kids decided that was going to be her nickname? Swotty Sophia. She let her hair down. But now it was all kinked and messy from the ponytail. Scruffy Sophia, she thought. That sounded even worse than Swotty Sophia. Her mother shouted from downstairs.

"Come on, Sophia! Don't want to be late on your first day!" Nothing else for it, Sophia tied her hair back into a ponytail, took a deep breath and trotted down the stairs.

Now can you feel Sophia's nerves? Can you feel the dread? I know I can, and I left school years ago. That is the power of showing instead of telling.

DON'T TELL THEM THAT THE MOON IS SHINING. SHOW THEM.

OK!

"DON'T TELL ME THE MOON IS SHINING; SHOW ME THE GLINT OF LIGHT ON BROKEN GLASS."

ANTON CHEKHOV

(FAMOUS RUSSIAN PLAYWRIGHT AND SHORT STORY WRITER.)

TELL DON'T SHOW:
A QUICK POINT ABOUT GETTING TO THE POINT

Now, as awesome as Show Don't Tell is (and it really is), there will be times when you need something that gets straight to the point. Sometimes you want your readers to know a piece, or several pieces, of information as quickly and simply as possible. This is when you use (in case you hadn't guessed) Tell Don't Show. Here's an example:

Isaac wasn't like other schoolboys. He didn't like fish fingers, he wore an expensive watch, and on Wednesdays he could travel through time. Unfortunately for Isaac, today was a Tuesday, he had maths and he'd forgotten to do his homework.

That's a whole lot of tell and absolutely no show. But it's fun, it's fast and – I hope – it captured your curiosity. The best writing uses a mixture of show and tell and, with practice, you and your Creative Monster will know which to use when.

TELL ME WHAT'S WHAT. SHOW ME WHAT YOU'VE GOT.

Write a scene that shows us a character is angry. First, decide why he or she is angry. Perhaps they have an annoying brother or sister. Maybe their parents have given them a long list of chores. Perhaps a friend has let them down.

We'll need to know some (but not necessarily all) of that information, so set the scene in one or two sentences of tell. Then show us their anger.

How you decide to demonstrate your character's anger is up to you. Except for one thing – you're not allowed to use the words mad, furious, irate or any other **synonyms*** for angry.

What are you still doing here? Go and make someone angry!

WHAT DOES THEIR FACE LOOK LIKE WHEN THEY LOSE THEIR TEMPER?

HOW DOES THEIR VOICE SOUND?

WHAT DO THEY DO WITH THEIR HANDS, FEET, BODY?

DO THEY THROW ANYTHING, BREAK ANYTHING, SLAM ANYTHING?

SHOW ME YOUR ANGRY FACE!!!

ERRR... GRRRRR?

*A SYNONYM is a word with the *same* or *similar* meaning to another word. Synonyms for silly are: daft, stupid, idiotic, crazy, bonkers.

An ANTONYM is the *opposite* of another word. Antonyms for silly are: sensible, responsible, wise, clever.

GIVE YOUR DESCRIPTIONS CLAWS
USING SIMILES TO MAKE YOUR WRITING SPARKLE

Description in a story is like claws on a monster. It grabs you, holds you, pulls you into the scene you are reading. Strong description makes characters and places more realistic, makes comedy funnier, drama more intense and danger more terrifying. One way of strengthening your descriptions is by using **similes**.

Similes are a way of describing one thing by comparing it to another. We do this using a joining word such as *like, as* or *resembled*. Here's an example:

The man's voice boomed *like* thunder.

Can you imagine what that voice sounds like? Loud, deep and rumbling. And isn't this simile more interesting than simply saying:

The man's voice was loud, deep and rumbling?

47

Here's another:

The porridge *resembled* a giant splodge of elephant snot.

How does that sound? Disgusting? I certainly hope so. Because instead of telling you the porridge was disgusting, I wanted you to *experience* that disgustingness for yourself (sorry!). That's what a good simile can do.

And one more:

His beard was *as* messy *as* a bird's nest.

Easy, right? But wait, similes can do more than describe something; they can also create a mood. I'll show you what I mean…

SUPERCHARGE YOUR SIMILES

A simile can be more effective if the comparison you use is a "good fit" for the thing or person you are describing. Let's start with a pair of red lips:

Her lips were as red as *rose petals.*

This simile would work fine for Snow White – someone beautiful, happy and caring. But if we are describing a witch – scary, wicked, creepy – the comparing word will be stronger if it matches her character. How about this?

Her lips were as red as *blood.*

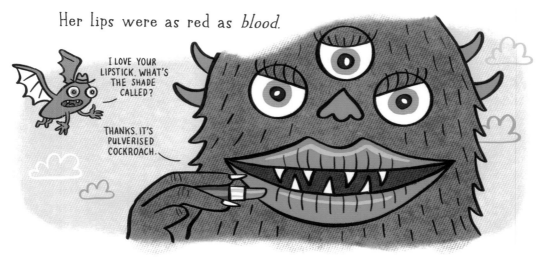

Not bad, certainly creepy, but not entirely original either. So, let's try one more time:

Her lips were the same shade of red as a *squashed bug.*

Much creepier. And much better for it. So pick your similes carefully. As well as helping you paint a picture, they can also create a deeper mood or feeling.

Right, let's create some similes of our own. I'll meet you at the next exercise.

SHOW ME YOUR ~~SIMILES~~ CLAWS

Open your notebook and see if you can
complete the following similes:

The giant was as tall *as…*

The girl was as strong *as…*

The teacher was furious. Clambering out
of the muddy stream, she *resembled* a…

When the ball hit him in the belly, it felt *like…*

Next, I want you to find a magazine, newspaper or book and
choose an interesting person to describe. Your character can be
human, animal or monster. They can look beautiful, weird or
frightening. Just so long as they look interesting.

You don't need to describe everything – in fact, it's better if you
concentrate on two or three key details and bring them to life with
strong similes. Similes that grab your readers and hold their attention.

Remember: a good simile can create a feeling; it can give your
readers clues about what kind of person your character is –
dangerous, heroic, silly or wise.

What are you waiting for? Go and get your claws out.

YOU'RE AS LONG
AND STRIPY
AND WIGGLY AS …

… CRAZY
TOOTHPASTE?

ADD BITE TO YOUR WRITING
MAKING A MARK WITH METAPHORS

If similes are like claws, then **metaphors** are fangs. They make your descriptions bite. By which, I mean they leave a lasting impression on your reader.

Metaphors are similar to similes (tongue-twister alert!). But where similes describe something as being *like* something else, metaphors describe something *as if it was* something else. Like this:

WHO ARE YOU CALLING A FAT DOLLOP OF CREAM?

SORRY, MOON.

> The moon *was* a fat dollop of cream, hanging in the night sky.

No it wasn't! Not *really*. But I bet you can see the moon more clearly than if I'd simply said: "The moon was big and round and white."

Metaphors are not literally true, but they help us *imagine* the thing being described in a fresh and interesting way. How about this:

> The story prompts in this book *are* tiny sparks that will ignite large fires.

Not *literally*. Your notebook will not burst into flames every time you write a story. (Well, I certainly hope not.) But this metaphor is a great way of describing the excitement we experience when we turn a small idea into a fully formed story.

COOL... I MEAN, HOT. I MEAN COOL... YOU KNOW WHAT I MEAN.

The classroom *was* a circus.

THIS ISN'T A CIRCUS OR A CLASSROOM. IT'S A METAPHOR.

Well, unless it was a circus school, then this isn't *literally* true. But it does suggest the classroom is noisy and chaotic.

All of these examples – of metaphors describing *things* – would work well as similes. However, when it comes to describing actions and people, I find metaphors work better.

For example, let's look at a metaphor to describe a boy who loves to read.

Metaphor: Sanjay gobbled up books.

Simile: Sanjay went through books as if he was gobbling them up.

Is it just me, or is the simile a bit awkward?

MMM. BOOKS!

I'M NOTHING LIKE YOU!

Let's try using metaphor to describe a character:

Metaphor: "My dad *is* a pig!" said Phoebe.

Simile: "My dad is *like* a pig!" said Phoebe.

To my ear, the word "like" softens the comparison and makes it less effective. Either way, Phoebe's father sounds terrible!

PLAYING WITH METAPHORS

A great metaphor is a wonderful thing. So when you find one, don't waste it. Instead, play with it, expand upon it, and use it throughout your story.

Let's return to Phoebe's father. The metaphor – "My dad is a pig!" – suggests he is messy, rude, noisy and smelly. In short, it tells us he is a slob! So let's play with that metaphor and turn those suggestions into actions on the page and images in our readers' minds. When Phoebe's dad eats, we can write:

He bent over his supper, his snout inches from the food, as if he was eating from a trough rather than a plate.

And if, for example, he puts his feet on the table, we can describe it like this:

Phoebe's dad leant back in his chair and placed his big smelly trotters on the table.

You can play with a metaphor as soon as you introduce it. And you can have fun with it at any point later on in your story. Just don't waste them! (The same goes for similes – squeeze every single drop of creativity out of those suckers.)

BIG FLUFFY METAPHORS

Open your notebook and write a metaphor to describe the sun on a hot summer's day. Not a simile (so no "like", "as" or "resembled"), but a way of talking about the sun as if it really were something else. Why not choose a big fluffy metaphor for the clouds as well?

And while you're at it, see if you can invent some metaphors to describe one (or more) of the characters below.

- Someone with a terrible temper
- A woman with tons of energy
- A boy who is very loud
- A teacher who is unusually large

If you find one you particularly like, play with it and write a few sentences that bring your metaphor to life.

WHAT YOU DOING?

COMING UP WITH METAPHORS LIKE...

THOSE CLOUDS ARE BALLS OF FLUFF IN THE SKY'S GREAT BIG BLUE BELLY BUTTON.

ONCE UPON A TIME
MAKING SENSE OF TENSES

Sorry about this, but I'm going to talk about **tenses**. But I'll be brief, I promise. And I'll try and include a flying saucer. Do we have a deal? Great, follow me...

In writing, there are three tenses, the **past tense**, the **present tense** and the **future tense**. But you look clever and I'm sure you know this already. I only mention tenses because I want you to remember that all three are available to you when you come to write a story.

You can write about something that happened in the past, something that is happening right now and something that is going to happen in the future.

The **past tense** reads like this:

Fiona *was sitting* in her garden, minding her own business, when a flying saucer *landed* in the middle of the lawn.

The past tense is effective because by telling us this thing has *already* happened … we are suggesting it *really* happened. That's why so many stories start with the words: *Once upon a time.*

This same sentence written in the **present tense** reads like this:

> Fiona *is sitting* in her garden, minding her own business, when a flying saucer *lands* in the middle of the lawn.

I like the present tense – it sounds very immediate and exciting. It makes us feel like we are a part of the story, seeing it unfold around us.

LOOK! A HUMAN TO ANNOY.

And using the **future tense**, we get this:

> Fiona *will be sitting* in the garden, minding her own business, when, all of a sudden, a flying saucer *will land* in the middle of her lawn.

This promise, of some exciting thing to come, is certainly intriguing. But it is an unusual choice, and I wouldn't recommend using it for an entire story. Because if it feels unusual to the reader, it is likely to distract them from your wonderful story.

And we wouldn't want that, would we?

MY NAME IS ALPHA-12. I AM FROM THE PLANET BLAH.

The future tense can be effective in small passages, in an introduction, perhaps, to grab the readers' attention and draw them into your story. Maybe something like this:

> Fiona *will* be sitting in the garden, minding her own business, when, all of a sudden, a flying saucer *will land* in the middle of her lawn. But for now, she *is* busy making breakfast, unaware that today *will be* the strangest day of her life.

I THINK WE'RE NEEDED ON THE NEXT PAGE, SUSAN.

A NOTE ON PAST, PRESENT AND FUTURE

The tense you *write* in (past, present, future) is not to be confused with when your story is actually *set*. For example, we can create a story set in ancient Egypt, but *written* in the present tense, like this:

> The Pharaoh wakes with the sunrise. Through his window, he sees the dark shapes of the half-built pyramids on the horizon.

And we can use the past tense to write a story set in the future, like this:

> It was the year 3021, robots had taken control of the world and humans lived in fear of their tyranny.

So have fun, play, experiment, be fearless. And if in doubt, stick with the old classic: *Once upon a time...*

STORY PROMPT
ALIENS IN THE GARDEN

The aliens from the previous example are too good to waste, so let's put them in a story. Think about who the main character is. What's their reaction to these visiting aliens – fear, excitement, confusion? What do the aliens want? And why did they land in this particular back garden? Oh, and what do they look like – this is a great opportunity for some descriptive writing.

One more thing before you start: which tense are you going to use?

OK, go and meet those aliens – they're waiting for you at the bottom of the garden.

LET'S TALK ABOUT TALKING
WRITING GREAT DIALOGUE

I love writing **dialogue** – those passages in a story where characters talk to one another. Or to their cat, or to themselves. When you get it right, dialogue reads easily and helps your story move quickly. It's also a great way of showing us what a character is like and of revealing important information to your readers.

"So how do you get dialogue right?" you ask.

"Well," I answer, "you start by *listening*."

"Listening? To what?"

"To the way people talk in real life. You'll notice it can be quite … how do I put this? Messy."

"Messy? *Whaddyamean*, messy?"

"People repeat themselves; they use unusual words."

"Like what?"

"Like 'whaddyamean'."

"Ah, I see."

"And they use ... *er* ... filler words, like *er* and *ah* and *um* and—"

"OK," you say, interrupting. "Messy dialogue, got it."

"But don't overdo it. It's important that your readers follow what's being said. And they need to know who's talking, so don't forget dialogue tags."

"Dialogue tags?"

"Yes," I say. "Dialogue tags – like *he said* and *she said*. Not after every line, just—"

"Now and then?"

"Exactly. You can use the occasional *he shouted*, or *she whispered*, but again—"

"Don't overdo it?"

"You're catching on fast," I say. "And remember that different characters have *different voices*. They have different ways of talking that reflect their personalities."

"For example?"

I scratch my chin while I think. "OK, one character might articulate their words with great precision, using elegant language and obscure words. Another might speak very quickly with their words coming one on top of the other, and repeating themselves with hardly any punctuation. Others are less talkative. And some might come from another country, so their English is a little ... how to say ... awkward."

"I like the sound of this dialogue," you say. "Maybe I should write some?"

"Great idea," I say. "Let's try an exercise."

IT'S GOOD TO TALK

"An exercise?" you say.

"Sure. Write a scene with three brothers trying to decide what to do on a rainy afternoon."

"Or sisters?"

"That works too. Think about their ages. Is one very young? Another more grown-up? Does one have a temper? Is one impatient? Is another funny? The dialogue should help us form an idea of the types of characters they are."

"Got it," you say, rubbing your hands together in excitement. You jump up and turn to go get your notebook and paper.

"Oh, and don't forget to add the occasional line of action," I say. "It helps to break up all the chat."

"Action," you say, running up the stairs to your room.

"It was good to talk," I say.

But you don't answer; instead I hear your bedroom door close and the sound of you sitting at your desk, eager to write a few pages of sparkling dialogue.

LEVEL 3
SECRET WEAPONS OF THE WORDSMITH

Just look at you and your Creative Monster!
I can sense the energy and story power crackling
through you. This monster training is really paying off.
But we're not finished yet. Welcome to Level 3.

This is where we take on some advanced writing
principles. Think of them as black belt techniques,
turning you and your Creative Monster into writing
ninjas. Wait, can a monster be a ninja? You know
what – with the tips and tricks contained in the
following pages, I think it can.

So sharpen your weapon (your pencil)
and leap into Level 3.

I'VE FILLED MY CHEKHOV'S GUN WITH ROWLING'S POTION.

CHEKHOV'S GUN AND ROWLING'S POTION
INTRODUCING IMPORTANT PEOPLE AND ESSENTIAL OBJECTS

Anton Chekhov was a Russian playwright and short story writer. He died over 100 years ago, but his stories are still considered to be some of the best ever written. He also left us a pretty cool writing principle. It's called Chekhov's gun, and it goes like this:

If someone places a gun on the table at the start of your story, then that gun had better get fired by the end. In other words, everything (and everyone) in your story should be there for a reason. Either right now, or later on. Otherwise, it's just taking up space.

A good way to appreciate this principle is to consider it in reverse: if a gun is needed to solve (or cause) a problem in your story, you should carefully introduce that gun earlier on. The same goes for keys, maps, magic potions, boats, ladders and anything else that your story calls for. Otherwise, if you have, for example, a key appear precisely when one is needed, then it all seems a bit ... well, lucky. The trick is to sneak the thing into your story at some earlier point. So it doesn't feel like cheating.

This is something J.K. Rowling does with great skill in the Harry Potter books. A spell or potion will be introduced in a playful or amusing way. But later, that same piece of magic will be used to major effect. But because you are familiar with the spell, you are excited – rather than frustrated – when it appears at a time of great importance. If you've read the books, go back and look at the way J.K. Rowling introduces items like Harry's Invisibility Cloak or Polyjuice Potion, and how these items become more important later on.

STORY PROMPT
"IT STARTED AS THE BEST DAY OF MY LIFE..."

First we need to set up the great day referred to in the title. Is it a party? Does someone win the lottery? What was so good about this day? You can establish all of this in one or two paragraphs.

And then, as the title suggests, something must go wrong. Exactly what that is will depend on how you start the story and just how mean you want to be to your character. (I would suggest very mean.)

Perhaps this is a story where you can practise the lesson from the previous page: hide something in the beginning that will come in useful at the end.

NOAH AND SCROOGE
ALLOW YOUR CHARACTERS TO GROW

You've heard of Charles Dickens, right? I mean, he's only one of the greatest writers ever to have held a quill. But why was he so good? Why are his stories as enjoyable today as they were almost 200 years ago? One reason (and there are many) is that he created wonderful characters. Like Ebenezer Scrooge, the **protagonist** (fancy word for "main character") of *A Christmas Carol*.

Scrooge was mean and miserable. He prized money above all else, and he despised Christmas. But over the course of the book, with the help of a few ghosts, Ebenezer learns the error of his ways. He learns the value of charity, compassion and good will. He even learns to love Christmas. In other words, he changes. And stories in which a character changes are highly satisfying. We call this change the **character arc.***

*When an object arcs, it changes direction. And when a CHARACTER ARCS, he or she changes the "direction" of their personality, for example, from scared to brave, from mean to kind.

66

We love to see characters grow: overcome fears, drop bad habits, change their opinions and become, as a result, better people. Characters can change a lot or a little, and it doesn't have to be limited to the hero of your story; your **supporting characters** (anyone other than the main character) can have arcs too.

Arcs can also work in the opposite direction, where a character moves from good to bad, creating a more tragic story.

But wait! I hear you say, what's all this got to do with Noah?

You remember the Bible story about Noah – massive flood, two of every animal? Well, Noah had a different kind of Ark. Noah's Ark (spelled with a "k", OK?) was a massive boat. But he didn't have a character arc (spelled with a "c", see?). Noah didn't change. He was the same at the end of the story as he was at the start (although his beard had probably grown quite a bit).

Does it mean the story of Noah's Ark isn't a good one? Not at all. All that rain and peril and boat-building, and all those animals being tossed about on the open seas (can you imagine the smell?!) – it's quite the adventure.

So what's the moral of the story? What can we learn from Noah and Scrooge? Let your characters grow; find a way to make them change. And if you can't give them an arc, give them a massive boat full of animals (or some similarly exciting experience).

"HAVE A LITTLE DAYDREAM ABOUT THE CHARACTER'S STORY, SEEING WHICH IDEAS FLOAT INTO THEIR MIND. IT'S IMPORTANT TO KNOW YOUR CHARACTERS PROPERLY BEFORE YOU START WRITING."

JACQUELINE WILSON
(AUTHOR OF THE TRACY BEAKER AND HETTY FEATHER STORIES.)

STORY PROMPT
BOYS AND GIRLS

Let's write a story based around a character arc. Before we begin, let's decide who our character is, and what will change over the course of two or three pages. Once you know those two things, you have the start and the end of your story. All you have to do then is write your way from one end to the other. Easy!

Choose one of the two character arcs below and then give yourself 30 minutes to turn it into a story.

1. A boy who won't play with girls, but then becomes best friends with … of all things, a girl!

2. A girl who is afraid of heights, but ends up being the best tree-climber in town.

WHAT'S THAT PONG?
DON'T FORGET THE SENSES

To make your writing feel real, to help your readers experience the story along with your characters, remember to use the senses – sight, smell, touch, sound and taste.

If a character is sitting in a (supposedly) quiet library, what can they hear? Pages turning, pens scratching on paper, a clock ticking? All of these details make the library feel more realistic.

If your character is at the beach, what do they smell? The salt from the sea, fish, suntan lotion? Can they smell a sunbather's skin turning brown?

In reality, no, but that doesn't stop you writing it. This is an example of **figurative writing**. Whilst it isn't literally true, it is vivid, dramatic and highly evocative.* This type of writing helps me feel the heat of the beach, helps me see the sunbather's skin glistening under the sun. It makes me feel like I'm there.

Here are some more figurative uses of the senses:

He could taste danger in the air.

She could feel the heat of the headmaster's anger.

He could hear the children's minds working.

Right, I smell an exercise coming up. Can you?

EXERCISE
A WALK THROUGH THE GRAVEYARD

A character is walking home from a birthday party. It's dark. The moon is high. They turn a corner and the road ahead is blocked, by a fallen boulder or tree. Maybe a flood. The only way home is to cut through the graveyard.

Write this scene, and be sure to use the senses. Describe the feel of the cold night air. What sounds can you hear? Animals, insects, a twig snapping? What else? How does the graveyard look in moonlight? Are there any smells? Describe it all, and watch out for ghosts!

I'M NOT SCARED.

I'M NOT SCARED.

I'M NOT SCARED.

RHYTHM
ADD VARIETY TO YOUR SENTENCES

Listen to this drumbeat:

DUM – DUM – DUM – DUM – DUM – DUM – DUM – DUM

What do you think? A bit repetitive? A bit boring? OK, how about this one:

DUM TSCH – DU-DU-DUM TSCH – DU-DU – DU-DU – DU-DU-DUM-TSCH?

– Much better, right?

The first version is nothing more than a monotonous beat, but the second has rhythm. Good writing has the same quality – it uses a mixture of sentence lengths to create a sense of rhythm. Long sentences that glide from left to right and line to line, pulling the reader along behind them. And short ones. To create variety. This gives your writing rhythm.

NEW PARAGRAPH → Punctuation helps as well – not only full stops and commas, but … ellipsis, dashes and (of course) brackets. And let's not forget paragraphs.

DASH

ELLIPSIS

COMMA

BRACKETS

FULL STOP

NEW PARAGRAPH → Before we read the words on the page, we see the page. We see the shape of the paragraphs, their black letters lined up in rows. And we see the spaces in between them. Spaces are important, because a page crammed full of words, with no paragraph breaks can be off-putting to even the most diligent bookworm. Long paragraphs are fine, but – for variety and rhythm – make sure to mix in a few short ones too.

So remember:

DUM TSCH — DU-DU-DUM TSCH — DUM TSCH — DU-DU-DUM TSCH — DU-DU—DU-DU—DU-DU-DU-DU-DU-DU-DUM-TSCH!

STORY PROMPT
THE WIND-UP MONKEY

Now, here's a scary story prompt for you. Just typing it out is giving me goosebumps. When I was little, I had a wind-up toy – a little plastic monkey that banged a pair of cymbals together. And it always gave me the creeps.

What if someone was given a toy just like this on their birthday? But because they had lots of other presents, they overlooked this particular toy. And then ... in the middle of the night – this boy or girl is woken by the sound of tiny banging cymbals: *tshh-tshh-tschh-tshh...*

This is where your story starts. You decide where it finishes. (And don't forget to use rhythm!)

I WOULDN'T SAY I'M EVIL, BUT I DO EAT BAKED BEANS STRAIGHT FROM THE TIN.

WHAT HAPPENS WHEN YOUR CHARACTER TURNS ON THE LIGHT? DOES THE MONKEY KEEP BANGING ITS CYMBALS, OR DOES IT ALL OF A SUDDEN STOP?

WHO GAVE THIS TOY TO YOUR CHARACTER?

IS THE WIND-UP MONKEY HAUNTED? CURSED? EVIL?

OR DOES YOUR CHARACTER SIMPLY HAVE AN OVERACTIVE IMAGINATION?

LET'S BE SPECIFIC
THE POWER OF DETAILS

Descriptive details can make scenes, characters and objects in your story feel more authentic.* I don't mean basic adjectives here, but specific details that can reveal, or suggest, something about our characters and the situations they find themselves in.

*AUTHENTIC means genuine or believable. Notice how it is similar to the word "author" – the writer of a book. In other words, a person who creates believable things.

An interesting thing happens when we write details, they make us – the writers – think more carefully about our stories and the people who inhabit them. These details feed our imagination and help us move the story forwards. Let's look at an example:

The man wore a jacket.

Well, fine. But don't we all?

76

The man wore a brown jacket.

The simple adjective – brown – is descriptive, but not particularly interesting or revealing.

The man wore a dusty brown jacket, slightly frayed around the collar.

Now we have something. The coat is vivid in my mind. And why is it frayed and dusty? Did the man have an accident? Fall through a hedge? Is he poor? Does he simply not care about appearances?

When you find a juicy detail, don't use it just once. Bring it back into your story later on – refer again to that frayed collar, the scar on someone's cheek, the noise a door makes when it opens. When you do this, your readers will recall the first time they read the detail, and the thing you are describing will feel familiar to them and, as a result, even more authentic. These details pull your readers deep into the story – just where you want them!

Little details, MONSTER difference.

77

WHERE DID THIS HAPPEN?

STORY PROMPT
THE DAY I NEARLY DROWNED

The key word here is "nearly", so we can assume our hero survives. But how? Well, that's entirely up to you. But you'd better be quick, that water looks cold!

And don't forget the details – they are the magic ingredients that can turn a good story into a great story.

You have 30 minutes.
Hurry, someone is cold and afraid and they need your help.

WAS YOUR CHARACTER ALONE OR WITH SOMEBODY?

DID THEY SAVE THEMSELVES, OR DID THEY NEED HELP?

DID THEY SLIP OR WERE THEY PUSHED?

HIT YOUR READERS OVER THE HEAD
DESCRIBING PHYSICAL SENSATIONS

When someone in our story experiences an intense physical sensation – pain, sickness, a wonderful bubble bath – we can help our reader share the characters' pleasure or pain, and bring them deeper into the world of our story. But that doesn't happen simply by telling the reader that:

Herni had flu and he felt absolutely dreadful.

The bubble bath was amazing.

Aliyah's headache was agonizing.

There are two problems with these descriptions:

1. They are common (we hear them all the time, so they have no special power).

2. They are not specific.

To make readers feel what our characters feel, we have to dig into the details. So let's take a closer look at Aliyah's "agonizing" headache, shall we?

⟶ She feels it in her head, sure, but where specifically? In her brain, in her temples, behind her eyes?

⟶ And what is the pain like? Does it throb, ache, stab, burn?

⟶ Do light and sound hurt? Does the pain make her sweat or cry out?

We don't need to answer all these questions, one or two juicy details will do. And then we get specific, we show instead of tell, we use similes and metaphors. We write something like this:

> Aliyah groaned as she pulled the blanket over her head. Her brain throbbed inside her skull, the pain spreading to her eyes and temples and neck. It felt as if her head was being squeezed in a giant fist. Her headache was agonizing.

I don't know about you, but I can feel that. I think I know what Aliyah is going through now, and I feel sorry for her. Maybe we can delete the last four words now ("Her headache was agonizing")? Or perhaps, in this instance, they work as a neat way of closing off the paragraph. What do you think?

SORRY, DID I SAY "BE THE STAR"? I MEANT "SEE STARS"!

MAKE SOMEONE SEASICK

See if you can write two or three sentences that make your readers feel seasick. They're on a rowing boat, a fishing trawler or an ocean cruiser when, all of a sudden, the skies turn grey, the wind picks up and the waves begin to churn. And your character turns a rather worrying shade of green.

All aboard? Jolly good, now let's go and make someone miserable.

NEOLOWHATNOTS

A WORD ABOUT UNUSUAL WORDS

Here's an unusual word for you: **neologism**. Just roll that around your mouth for a moment – ne-oloj-ism. Delicious, isn't it? It means a new word. Or a made-up word. And they can add real pizzazz (a real word, but lovely, nonetheless) to your writing.

Roald Dahl was wonderful at this, creating such words as "whizzpoppers" (farts), "snozzcumbers" (disgusting vegetables) and "chiddlers" (children). William Shakespeare and Charles Dickens were at it too: Shakespeare invented the word "bedazzled", and Mr Dickens gave us "the creeps". And if neologisms were good enough for Dahl, Dickens and Shakespeare, they're good enough for us.

But two notes of caution:

First: it's important that your reader understands what you are trying to say. So invent your words carefully and make sure the context (the rest of the sentence or paragraph) helps your reader get the word's meaning. It also helps if your neologism bears some similarity to the word (or words) it is replacing.

Like this:

> The boy began to dance – he wiggled his hips, waved his arms and nodded his head in time with the music. It was totally groovulous.*

*From groovy and fabulous – made up by me, just now.

Second: as with many of the ideas in this book, a little goes a long way – so have fun and be creative, but don't overdo it with the neolowhatnots.

83

WRITING WRONGS
THE IMPORTANCE OF EDITING

There's a great saying about writing, it goes like this: get it written, then get it right.

The process of getting a story right is called **editing**. But before you do any editing, there's something else you should do with your story first – absolutely nothing.

Once you've finished the **first draft** of a story, resist the temptation to read it straightaway. Put it down. Put it in a drawer. Lock the drawer. Hide the key. Go outside and play. Draw a picture. Eat some cake. Start a new story if you want. Anything. Just leave this story alone. Until tomorrow…

OK, it's tomorrow. Time to read that story through. Read it slowly and enjoy what you have created. Then, pick up a red pen and read it again, this time making marks when you find anything that needs fixing. And you will find plenty. Unless you're a genius. In which case, I look forward to reading your novel very soon.

For the rest of us, editing is where we take our story to the next level. How do we do that? You read my world-famous (well, not yet, but maybe one day) Editing Checklist. It's over there on page 88.

A FEW WORDS ABOUT "DRAFTS"

The **first draft** is a finished version of your story, before you do any editing. It will contain mistakes, maybe a few boring bits, a little repetition and perhaps some repetition.

So you do a **second draft**, fixing mistakes, tightening the writing, improving the story.

When your story is finished, when it's fixed, you have a **final draft**. Also known as a completely awesome story.

ERRRR, YOU'VE MADE MY HOUSE OUT OF JELLY.

WOBBLE!

DON'T WORRY, IT'S ONLY THE FIRST DRAFT.

"THE FIRST DRAFT OF ANYTHING IS RUBBISH."
ERNEST HEMINGWAY

(MR HEMINGWAY ACTUALLY USED A RUDE WORD INSTEAD OF "RUBBISH", BUT AS THIS IS A BOOK FOR CHILDREN, WE'LL STICK WITH "RUBBISH". HE ALSO WON THE NOBEL PRIZE FOR LITERATURE, SO HE KNEW HIS STUFF.)

AN EDITING CHECKLIST

1. **Fix the spelling and grammar.** Obviously!

2. **Do the characters' names stay the same throughout the story** (you'd be amazed how often they change)?

3. **Do they learn a lesson,** overcome a fear, grow as a person?

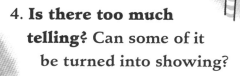

4. **Is there too much telling?** Can some of it be turned into showing?

5. **Is it too easy?** The goal, I mean – that thing that powers your story? Does the hero get what she wants too easily? Can you introduce more problems? Can you make her struggle just a little more?

6. **Are all your objects and characters really necessary?** If any are just hanging out taking up space, consider cutting them.

7. **Pay attention to your dialogue.** Do the characters have different ways of talking, or do they all sound the same?

8. **Does it make sense?** Sounds obvious, doesn't it? But read carefully – would the hero really do that? Would the plan really work?

IT LOOPED AIMLESSLY THROUGH THE SKY LIKE A BUTTERFLY ON ITS DAY OFF.

9. Can you add in any descriptive writing? Can you turn "a nice sunset" into: "the sun sat low on the horizon, painting the night sky in bold swathes of gold and violet"?

10. But don't overdo it! Don't let too much description slow your story down or get in the way of the action.

11. Are your similes supercharged? Did you play with your metaphors?

12. Does your writing have – *dum tsch – du-du-dum tsch* – **rhythm?**

13. Did you get specific to make your characters feel more realistic? Did you use details to help us feel what they are feeling?

REMEMBER TO GIVE IT RHYTHM!

I'M TURNING THE BORING BITS INTO SOMETHING NOT-BORING.

14. Did you remember to use the senses: sight, smell, touch, sound and taste?

15. Are there any boring bits? Cut them out or turn them into not-boring bits.

MIND YOUR STEP

Welcome to the middle of the book! You've completed Levels 1–3 of monster training – your plots are awesome, your characters leap off the page and your descriptions are electrifying.

So now that you know what works, let's take a look at what doesn't. Let's talk about mistakes. Everyone makes them – even your best friend, even your parents and teachers, even … Creative Monsters. And that's a good thing! If you're making mistakes, it means you're making something. It means you're writing, you're experimenting, you're being creative.

Sometimes, what looks like a mistake turns out to be an act of creative genius. And other times, a mistake is just a mistake – something we can fix to make our story better.

Follow me into the next section, and be careful not to step on any mistakes.

MONSTERS NEED EXERCISE
DON'T DO NOTHING

Some people say that if you're serious about being a writer, you should write every day. To those people, I blow a big fat raspberry. I don't want writing to be a chore for you. I want it to be fun. But if you want to write the very best stories you can (and that's what we're here for, right?), then I would encourage you to write regularly. Maybe once a week. Maybe more. The trick is to find your "Goldilocks" routine: not too little, not too much, but just right.

But remember this: the more you practise, the better you will become. So whatever you do, *don't do nothing.*

How many times will you write this week? Write it in your notebook: This week I will write ___ times.

Don't worry if you fall short, that's all part of figuring out a routine you can stick to.

93

SLOW STARTS
GET YOUR STORY GOING

~~Sometimes it can take time for a story to get warmed up. We, the writers, might spend the first page setting the scene and figuring out what we want to write. This is particularly true when we are working to a time limit.~~

Once you have finished your story, you will often find that it can be improved by getting rid of the first paragraph, or even page, and jumping straight into the action. This principle is known as *in media res*, which is Latin for "into the middle of things".

Say we are writing a story about a man shipwrecked on a desert island. We could begin the story with the man packing his bags at home. We learn he is an archaeologist, travelling to Egypt.

> MAYBE YOU SHOULD CUT THIS AND JUMP RIGHT IN?

Next we show him board the ship, move into his cabin, eat supper and go to bed. Then he wakes in the night with the ship lurching about on the waves, people screaming, an alarm sounding. The ship capsizes and the man is dumped into the water. He bangs his head and blacks out. Next thing he knows, he wakes up – bashed and confused – on the shore of the island.

But what if we cut that set-up, and begin the story with the man waking up in his cabin amid the storm and the chaos. Much better, don't you think? Certainly for a short story.

"TRY TO LEAVE OUT THE PART THAT READERS TEND TO SKIP."

(IN OTHER WORDS, DON'T BE BORING!)

ELMORE LEONARD

AUTHOR AND SCREENWRITER OF WESTERNS, CRIME STORIES AND OTHER THRILLING TALES.

STORY PROMPT
SHIPWRECKED

Let's wash someone up on a desert island, shall we?

He is lost, injured and frightened. He needs to find food and shelter, build a fire, build a boat. Perhaps there are dangerous animals and bloodsucking insects. Are there any other survivors from the shipwreck? Will he make it off the island alive?

As your story unfolds, you can drop in any details that are relevant and interesting. Who the man is, what he was doing on the ship and where he was going. But don't rush, take your time as you – and your character – explore this mysterious island.

Before you begin, take a minute to decide where you will start. On the ship amid the storm? Or with our hero already washed up on the golden sands of the island?

WHAT A MESS!
AVOID MIXING YOUR METAPHORS

Earlier, we talked about the benefits of playing with metaphors. But I forgot to warn you about the dangers of mixing them – it can make the most awful mess. Allow me to demonstrate:

Metaphor 1 (for an angry teacher):

> The teacher exploded.

Playing with metaphor 1:

> The teacher exploded. Her face went red, her voice boomed and the children all hid under their desks.

MONSTER METAPHOR!

I FEEL THEIR PAIN!

Metaphor 2 (when something ruins the mood):

> Their spirits were dampened.

Playing with metaphor 2:

> Their spirits dampened, the children flopped in their seats like wet leaves.

Now let's mix them:

The teacher exploded, which thoroughly dampened everybody's spirits.

Wait, what? How does an explosion dampen anything? It just doesn't work. It makes no sense. It's crazy, I tell you. Crazy!

So now you know – play with metaphors, but mix them at your peril!

MUDDLED MIDDLES
HOW TO KEEP YOUR STORY MOVING

Have you ever opened a box of chocolates and been so overwhelmed with options that you couldn't decide which one to pick? I know I have. Well, the middle of a story can be like that too. As your story progresses from a great opening, through the first few scenes and pages, *stuff* happens. Characters are created, mysteries raised and goals chased. Obstacles appear, rivalries form and *stuff* piles up. These piles of stuff are called FSPs – short for Fantastic Story Possibilities.

FSPs are what keep your story moving and your reader interested. But too many FSPs can be overwhelming. They can muddle the middle of your story. And muddled middles are no fun to write and less fun to read.

So be careful only to introduce characters and events that are important to your story. Yes, we all love unicorns, but if your story doesn't need one, best to save it for another story.

Inevitably, there will come a time when you have a choice of FSPs and can't decide which to use next. Don't worry; I'm here to help.

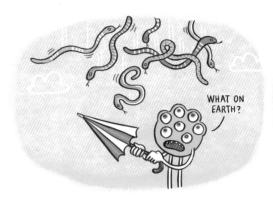

TO CHOOSE YOUR NEXT FSP, ASK:

- ⟾ Which creates the most excitement?
- ⟾ Which challenges your hero the most?
- ⟾ Which is most surprising?
- ⟾ Which causes the most trouble?

You will get different answers to different questions, but the process of examining your FSPs will help you see which are strongest. And if you are still stuck, there is one more question to ask: which is most fun to write?

This is almost always the right way to go. And if it's not? That's the beauty of writing stories instead of building skyscrapers. If the middle of a story (or the start, or the end, for that matter) isn't working, you can take it out and try something different. Taking the middle out of a skyscraper, however, is a very messy business.

EXERCISE
FIND THE FSPs

Time to do some reading. Whatever book you're enjoying at the moment (because I assume you are reading something, right?), I want you to take it somewhere quiet and read for 30 minutes. But I want you to take a notepad and pencil with you, and every time you spot an FSP, I want you to write it down. By the time your 30 minutes are up, you should have several FSPs.

Then, I want you to pick one and run with it. Not literally run around the house waving your notebook in the air, but sit down and write a few paragraphs or pages that follow on from that Fantastic Story Possibility.

GETTING STUCK INSIDE YOUR CHARACTER'S HEAD
TURNING THOUGHTS INTO ACTION

Being able to read a character's thoughts – to know what they are worrying about, what they are planning and what they remember – is one of the delights of written stories (this sort of thing is difficult to do in films).

But spending too much time inside a character's head can become boring for your readers. Like this:

Dave sat at the kitchen table, thinking about his band at school. They were good. With one significant exception – their drummer was terrible. Mike just sat behind the drums and banged them randomly. If they wanted to win Battle of the Bands, they would have to drop Mike and find someone who could really play. But if he kicked Mike out of the band, would the two of them be able to stay friends? But if he didn't, wouldn't that be unfair to the other band members? He didn't know what to do.

103

The previous paragraph contains plenty of good story information, but it's not a particularly exciting scene. Much better to get those thoughts out in the open, to give our character someone to discuss their thoughts with. Someone who can agree, disagree, offer good advice or bad. This creates action and the possibility for drama (an argument) or comedy (a misunderstanding), or any number of interesting scenes. It depends on who your character talks to, so choose their interlocutor* carefully. It can be their best friend, a parent, a total stranger. It can even be a ... dog.

*Fancy word for talk partner.

Dave paced up and down the kitchen. He always paced when he had a problem. And right now he had a big one: whether or not to kick the drummer – and Dave's best friend – out of their band.

"What do you think, Jack?"

Jack looked up from the bone he was chewing. He licked his lips.

"No," said Dave. "I'm not sure either."

Jack stretched, then began nibbling at his tail.

"I know he's my best friend," Dave said. "But he's a terrible drummer."

Jack wagged his tail, making it beat time on the floor.

"Exactly," said Dave. "You're a better drummer than he is. It's not fair on the rest of the band, is it?"

Jack rolled over to have his tummy tickled. Dave knelt down and did what was required. Jack woofed.

"I know!" said Dave. "We'd have a real chance of winning if we had a decent drummer. But…"

Jack yawned.

"OK, OK," said Dave. "I can take a hint. I'll call a band meeting tonight and tell him. It's going to be awful."

Jack made a low gruffing sound.

"I hope you're right. I hope he does understand."

Jack took the bone with his mouth and wandered off into the garden.

"Thanks for the chat," Dave said. "It really helped."

Clearly Dave is a little bonkers, but he's more interesting for it. And I really hope he works things out with Mike.

EXERCISE
CHICKEN OR MANGO?

Let's write a scene about a character making a big decision. A really big, life-changing decision. Like … what to have for supper.

OK, it's not really life-changing – well, unless someone has poisoned the chicken. So yes, let's go with that – the character is trying to decide between a chicken pie (that, unbeknownst to him has been poisoned), and a mango salad.

You could write this scene entirely inside the character's head as he weighs up all the pros and cons of a chicken pie and a mango salad.

But we're not going to do that. We're going to turn this decision into action.

This might be as simple as the character taking the food out of the fridge and – smelling it, prodding it, inspecting it – voicing his thoughts out loud.

Or maybe there is someone else in the scene, someone with whom he can talk and debate the options.

WHY WOULD THE PIE BE POISONED? MAYBE YOUR CHARACTER IS A SECRET AGENT, A KING, OR A RUTHLESS BILLIONAIRE. FOR THIS EXERCISE, IT ISN'T CRUCIAL THAT YOU KNOW, BUT THESE DETAILS COULD MAKE YOUR SCENE MORE INTERESTING. HOWEVER, IF YOU ARE TEMPTED TO TURN THIS INTO A COMPLETE STORY, THEN THESE ARE DETAILS YOU WILL ABSOLUTELY NEED TO KNOW.

HI, I'M THE SNOW MONSTER FROM THE BEGINNING OF THIS BOOK, AND WHEN I'M NOT OUT SCARING MOUNTAINEERS, YOU'LL FIND ME ARRANGING FLOWERS, OR VOLUNTEERING AT MY LOCAL ANIMAL SANCTUARY.

AND I MAY LOOK LIKE A MILD-MANNERED AUTOGRAPH COLLECTOR, BUT I'M ACTUALLY AN INTERNATIONAL SPY WITH A BLACK BELT IN TAEKWONDO.

COOKIE-CUTTER CHARACTERS
ORIGINAL* HEROES AND UNCONVENTIONAL** VILLAINS

When you use a cookie cutter, all the cookies come out looking the same – circular, star-shaped, heart-shaped, depending on the cutter. Good for cookies. Not so good for characters, who should be varied and unpredictable.

A cookie-cutter hero, for example, would be handsome, strong and charming. And a cookie-cutter baddy might be ugly, scrawny and temperamental.

We've seen these types of heroes and villains in many films and books. And, well, it's kind of boring, don't you think?

*ORIGINAL means new. Something created by you, rather than a copy of something else.

**UNCONVENTIONAL means unexpected, unusual, and not made with a cookie cutter.

107

So let's mix it up when we create our heroes and villains. Let's show some diversity and imagination.

How about a princess who likes to wrestle?

Or a hero in a wheelchair?

An assassin who reads poetry?

A wise man who lifts weights?

Have fun with your characters. But leave the cookie cutter in the kitchen, and create someone original.

EXERCISE
APPEARANCES CAN BE DECEPTIVE

Invent a character whose appearance is not at all like their
personality. How might a total stranger react to them –
based purely on the way they look?

First of all, think about your character's appearance.

✏⇨ Does your character look scary or kind?
✏⇨ Do they look brainy or silly?
✏⇨ Are they big or small?
✏⇨ Neat or scruffy?
✏⇨ Do they have tattoos, jewellery,
muscles, glasses, a scar,
a limp, a top hat?

Once you've decided, write a scene
introducing that person to a
stranger or group of strangers.
And let's see how they react.

> HOW ABOUT A
> FIRST DAY AT SCHOOL?
>
> OR MAYBE YOUR CHARACTER
> IS VISITING ANOTHER PLANET?
>
> OR (I LIKE THIS ONE) YOUR
> CHARACTER ACCIDENTALLY
> BUMPS INTO SOMEONE, CAUSING
> THAT PERSON TO SPILL A DRINK
> ALL OVER THEIR CLOTHES.

OOOPS.
SORRY!

SWING

FLOPPY ENDINGS
BUILDING TO A STRONG FINISH

You've worked so hard on your story; you've created an exciting start, invented great characters and given them numerous obstacles to overcome. It's funny, dramatic, terrifying, thrilling! It would be a shame to ruin all that work with a weak, disappointing and generally floppy ending.

So first things first (or should that be last things first?): resist the temptation to rush. Draw out the final battle, make your hero struggle one last time or throw in a last-minute twist. Keep your reader guessing until the very end.

Also – like grabbing your bags before getting off a bus – don't leave any story luggage behind before you get off your writing chair.

If you left a cat stuck up a tree, get it down.

If there is an unexploded bomb anywhere, defuse it.

If two characters are attracted to each other, allow them to kiss.

If someone made a promise, make sure they keep it.

Or, don't. You don't have to conclude all your story elements in a positive way – by all means, leave the cat up the tree, or stop the couple from having that smooch. But do pay them one last visit before you type "The End". The effect can be funny, or dramatic, or sad – so long as the reader knows you didn't forget about it, they will accept whatever version you write.

FOUR WAYS TO END A STORY

There are many ways to end a story, an infinite number of ways, but you can usually place the ending into one of four categories. Here they are:

UPBEAT

YOU KNOW, THE GOOD GUY WINS, THE WORLD IS SAVED, THE CONTEST WON AND EVERYONE LIVES HAPPILY EVER AFTER.

DOWNBEAT

THE HERO DOES NOT WIN, JUSTICE IS NOT SERVED, TRAGEDY HAPPENS, LOVE IS LOST, THE UNTHINKABLE HAPPENS.

BITTERSWEET

AS THE NAME SUGGESTS, THIS ENDING COMBINES GOOD AND BAD. PERHAPS THE WORLD IS SAVED BUT, IN THE PROCESS, THE HERO IS KILLED. OR SOMEONE LOSES ALL THEIR MONEY, BUT FINDS LOVE.

UNRESOLVED

MAYBE THE VILLAIN IS DEFEATED, BUT NOT CAPTURED. PERHAPS THERE IS A HINT THAT THE GOOD GUY HAS A DARK SECRET. THESE ARE THE ENDINGS THAT KEEP YOU GUESSING.

EXERCISE

AN ALTERNATIVE ENDING

I'd like you to revisit one of the stories you have written so far. One you loved. Or maybe one that you weren't so sure about. And then I'd like you to write a different ending – if the original ending was happy, try writing a sad ending, or a bittersweet ending. If the original ending was downbeat, see if you can make it happy, or give it an unresolved ending that keeps the reader guessing.

Read your original story to a friend or someone from your family. And then try the new ending on them and ask which they prefer.

WHAT ARE YOU DOING?

I NEED TO GO TO THE SHOPS, BUT I ALSO REALLY WANT TO FINISH WRITING MY STORY.

"FINISH WHAT YOU'RE WRITING. WHATEVER YOU HAVE TO DO TO FINISH IT, FINISH IT."

NEIL GAIMAN

(AUTHOR OF BOOKS FOR ADULTS AND CHILDREN, MANY OF WHICH HAVE WON PRIZES AND BEEN TURNED INTO MOVIES.)

SMASHING THROUGH WRITER'S BLOCK

Imagine the scene: your pencil is a blur as you write one exciting line after another, then – all of a sudden – your pencil stops moving. Your characters don't know what to do with themselves. And your story grinds to a halt. You've hit the dreaded Writer's Block.

But you're not alone. It happens to all writers sooner or later. Charles Dickens? He got as blocked as a Victorian sewer. J.K. Rowling? As blocked as a troll's nose in flu season. Roald Dahl? As blocked as the tubes in a chocolate factory. They all got blocked.

And they all got unblocked, too. So, when it happens to you, don't panic, you're in good company. Relax, and read through the tips on the following pages about how to break through Writer's Block and get your story moving forward.

OUTLINING
PLANNING YOUR STORY BEFORE YOU START WRITING

Some writers like to discover their stories as they write them – making them up as they go along. This is what we are doing when we write our stories quickly, to a time limit. Other writers prefer to know where they are going before they set off on their story adventure. The process of figuring this out is called **outlining**.

Think about the way you might draw the outline of, say, a monster, before colouring it in. Getting the shape and size right, putting the eyes in the right place, deciding on the number of legs, tentacles and heads. And if it's not right, we fix the outline before we reach for the coloured pens.

MY OUTLINE LOOKS PERFECT. YOU CAN COLOUR ME IN NOW. QUICK – I FEEL NAKED!

ERRR, I'M NO EXPERT, BUT THOSE HORNS LOOK UPSIDE DOWN. HERE, YOU MIGHT NEED THIS.

JEFF GREY

Outlining a story is kind of similar. We give our story a shape before we start to write. We think about lots of different story ideas and plot points* and then decide which are best before we start writing all the sentences, paragraphs and pages that make up our fully formed story.

Not all of your ideas will work – some will be too complicated, some too boring, others too crazy. But if you persevere, it won't take long to come up with enough ideas to create an original and exciting story. Your outline will serve as a kind of story map, stopping you and your Creative Monster from getting lost as you write your way towards the end.

I've written an example outline on the next few pages to give you an idea of how it works. Notice how the plot points are usually obstacles or the steps my character takes to solve them. Also notice that sometimes I came up with several ideas before finding one I liked. But that is the whole point of outlining.

*Plot points are explained on page 26 "Avalanche!"

ALL HE WANTED WAS A GLASS OF LEMONADE

AN EXAMPLE STORY OUTLINE

WHO IS MY CHARACTER AND WHAT IS THEIR GOAL?

~~A writer wants to win a writing contest with a £100 prize.~~

~~An evil genius wants to steal all the animals from the zoo.~~

A boy called Ethan wants a glass of lemonade.

PLOT POINT 1

~~Ethan finds lemonade but can't find a glass.~~

~~Ethan's lips get stuck together and he can't drink.~~

Ethan goes to the fridge – there is no lemonade.

THE THING YOUR CHARACTER WANTS DOESN'T HAVE TO BE EXOTIC OR EXTRAORDINARY. SIMPLE THINGS (LIKE WANTING A GLASS OF LEMONADE) CAN BE ENOUGH SO LONG AS THE CHARACTER HAS TO STRUGGLE TO GET THEM.

PLOT POINT 2

~~He drinks milk instead.~~

He decides to buy lemonade with money from his piggy bank.

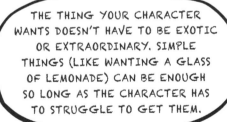

PLOT POINT 3

~~He can't find his piggy bank.~~

There is only 50p in his piggy bank.
A can of lemonade costs £1.00.

PLOT POINT 4

Ethan goes looking
for more money.

He empties all his drawers.

He rummages through
all his pockets.

He looks down the
back of the sofa.

PLOT POINT 5

He only finds another 35p.
He's still 15p short of £1.00.

PLOT POINT 6

Ethan goes to the shop anyway and asks if he can have the lemonade now then come back with the rest of the money tomorrow.

PLOT POINT 7

The shopkeeper says no.

PLOT POINT 8

~~Ethan steals the lemonade.~~

~~Ethan pretends to cry, hoping the shopkeeper will feel sorry for him.~~

The shopkeeper offers Ethan a job delivering newspapers. He'll pay £4.00 plus a can of lemonade. Ethan agrees.

PLOT POINT 9

The shopkeeper tells him to watch out for Number 12 Acorn Avenue. The man who lives there reckons he's a wizard.

NEXT STEPS

Ethan sets off on his bike and arrives at Number 12 Acorn Avenue. What happens once he gets there? Right now, I honestly don't know. But I have a feeling it is going to involve a man wearing a pointy hat.

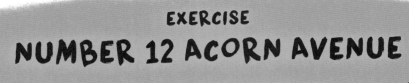

EXERCISE
NUMBER 12 ACORN AVENUE

Finish my outline. Ethan stops his bicycle in front of
Number 12 Acorn Avenue. But what happens next?
What is Ethan's goal at this point in the story?

✏➤ To get home quickly and, finally, enjoy his can of lemonade?
✏➤ To find out if the man at Number 12 really is a wizard?
✏➤ All of the above?
✏➤ Or something completely different?

Once you're happy with your outline,
why not sit down and write this story?

REMEMBER, YOU CAN
START ANYWHERE YOU LIKE.
WITH ETHAN LOOKING FOR
LEMONADE, OR (REMEMBER THE
SECTION CALLED "SLOW STARTS"
ON PAGE 94?) MAYBE WE BEGIN
WITH ETHAN ROLLING UP
OUTSIDE NUMBER 12.
IT'S UP TO YOU.

GET CRAZY!
THE POWER OF UNPREDICTABILITY

You're stuck. You think of all kinds of things that could happen, but none of them feel right. Maybe they're too predictable* – too obvious, too boring. So what do you do?

Write something unpredictable, of course. Write a list of all the things your character would not do. All the things his friends and enemies would not do. All the things that would not happen. Write a great big list of crazy.

Then you see if there is any possible way you can make one of these crazy things happen. But be careful, there is a fine line between unpredictable and unbelievable.

*When something is PREDICTABLE, it means we can see it coming. We know what to expect. This is a good quality in pizza restaurants. But a disaster for stories.

For example, a little old lady is unlikely to defeat a cat burglar in a fist fight – but she might try, if we have established that she is brave. And a downpour of frogs is certainly unpredictable, but is it believable?*

If nothing on your list passes the believability test, then is there something similar that does? If not an explosion, maybe a fire? If not a fire, have someone burn the toast. If not a rampaging werewolf, how about a rabid dog? Or a lost puppy? All of these things are interesting, all have consequences and they can all get your story moving again.

*Part of a writer's job is making the unbelievable BELIEVABLE. So anything is possible. You just need a "reason why". If you give your readers a good reason to believe, they will follow you anywhere. Even into a downpour of frogs.

STORY PROMPT
THE DAY IT RAINED FROGS

Imagine sitting in your garden, minding your
own business, when … splat! A frog drops into your lap.
Or on your head or into your bowl of ice cream.
Then another, then another, and then … it's raining frogs.

Imagine the chaos. People screaming, frogs jumping,
traffic screeching to a halt.

What happens next? Where do the frogs go? Who takes control?

And – most importantly – where did all those frogs come from?
This is the "reason why" mentioned in the tiny blob on the
previous page. If you can figure that out, you have a story.

So go and get figuring. Then get writing.
And you might want to take an umbrella.

WHAT'S THE POINT?
FIND A THEME AND LET IT GUIDE YOU

A good way to get a story unstuck is to see if you can find a **theme**. A theme is the message, moral or idea buried inside your story. Not all stories have them, but many of the best do. And some have several.

Take *The Lord of the Rings* books. On the surface, they're about a bunch of hobbits on a mission to destroy an evil ring. But at a deeper level, these stories are about bravery, friendship, respecting the environment and the idea that ordinary folk can achieve extraordinary things.

Here are some examples of themes from stories you may know:

With great power comes great responsibility
– Spider-Man by Stan Lee & Steve Ditko

Good things happen to good children
– Charlie and the Chocolate Factory by Roald Dahl

It's OK to be different
– The Boy in the Dress by David Walliams

Being a child can be tough
– Where the Wild Things Are by Maurice Sendak

Sometimes, we know what the theme is before we start writing. Other times, we simply have a great idea for a story. But that doesn't stop us from deciding on a theme later on.

Let's look at an example:

It's the day of a big dance contest and Sonja has a good chance of winning. Or should that be *had* a good chance of winning. Following an argument with her sister (in which an expensive dress was torn), Sonja has been grounded. She's practised all year long for this contest, but now she's stuck in her room.

And you are stuck at your desk, trying to decide what happens next. So let's look for a theme and see if we can get our story moving again.

How about these:

- Big sisters are evil.
- Grown-ups are unfair.
- Pursue your dreams at all costs.
- Bad tempers make bad decisions.

I SAW IT FIRST!

All of these are good, and all will point your story in a slightly different direction. I like the theme – the idea – "Bad tempers make bad decisions". So how does this theme guide our story?

Let's invent some other plot points based on our theme:

Sonja could kick a door and break her toe. Bad temper, bad decision, see?

She might throw her shoe at the door, just as her mother is coming into the room to give her one last chance. The shoe hits her mother in the head.

She could climb out of the window, get spotted by the police and be arrested on suspicion of being a burglar. *This idea also explores the theme "Pursue your dreams at all costs".*

Or maybe we look at our theme in reverse: Sonja handles her punishment with calm and grace (a good decision) and is rewarded. *This is an example of a character arc, as discussed in the section "Noah and Scrooge" on page 66.*

Whichever option you choose, your story is now moving in the right direction, which is to say forwards. Think of themes as peanuts coated in chocolate.* Often the chocolate is enough, but a hidden peanut can make all the difference.

CHOCOLATE = STORY   PEANUT = THEME

SALIVATING MONSTER = SALIVATING MONSTER

* For those who don't like peanuts, think of themes as chocolate-coated raisins. If you don't like raisins, then I'm sorry, there's nothing I can do for you.

STARTING WITH A THEME

We've talked about using themes to help you when you get stuck in the middle of a story. But they can also be used for coming up with new story ideas. Think about a moral or message that interests you, and then create characters and events to bring that theme to life.

Below is a list of themes that could lead to exciting stories. Choose one, or think of your own, and then turn it into a story. And if at any point you get stuck, use your theme to help you come up with ideas for what happens next.

Some themes:

⟸⟹ Hard work is more important than talent.
⟸⟹ Money can't buy happiness.
⟸⟹ We can learn a lot from animals.
⟸⟹ Adults don't always know what's best.
⟸⟹ Sometimes you have to do the wrong thing
for the right reason.

Because this one requires some extra thought, you can have 45 minutes. Aren't I generous? Now, off you go.

THEME:

Never judge a monster by its claws

A KNOCK AT THE DOOR
INTRODUCE A NEW CHARACTER

Sometimes, when the action slows down and your hero runs out of ideas, a new character can give your story the shove it needs to get going again. Someone with new information, perhaps. An old enemy or a new friend. New characters can bring energy to your story: interesting ideas, danger, love, fear. It all depends on who they are.

But don't invite any old character into your story. Think about why you're stuck and what your hero is trying to achieve. Can the new character help? Or maybe your story is stuck because you need a problem for your hero to struggle against. In which case, the new character should bring – or be – that problem.

So have a new character (or someone from earlier in the story) knock at the door, crash through the window or parachute into the middle of the action.

THE DAY MUM WENT BONKERS

I'm sure you'll have plenty of fun sending Mum bonkers, and thinking of all the crazy things she could do. And all the ways her family or friends react to this unusual behaviour. But once you have set the scene and sent Mum crazy, see if you can introduce a new character that will move the story forwards? A doctor, a teacher, a neighbour, the police, somebody else? Choose carefully then get that character to knock on the door.

Right, you've got 30 minutes to drive your mum crazy. Get to it!

WHY DID MUM — NORMALLY SO COOL AND IN CONTROL — GO BONKERS?

WAS IT A REACTION TO EXTRAORDINARILY GOOD NEWS? OR BAD?

DID SHE BANG HER HEAD?

WAS SHE UNDER A SPELL?

DID SHE STAY BONKERS, OR WAS SHE ABLE TO RETURN TO NORMAL?

BACKWARDS SPEAKING ONLY I'M, ON NOW FROM.

WHAT ON EARTH?

GET DIGGING
SEARCH YOUR STORY FOR USEFUL DETAILS

Often, the answer to a story problem is hidden in the story itself. So if you get stuck (and, as we know, you will), put down the pencil and pick up your pages. Find a comfortable chair and read what you've written so far. Read carefully and – like a pirate on a beach – look for buried treasure.*

Is there a friend we forgot about? A talent, a fear or a weakness? Is there a gun on the mantelpiece, a creaky floorboard, a hidden door, a bicycle leaning up against a lamp post? If there is, then find a way to use it.

If there isn't, decide what you need, then go back and bury it in the sands of your beginning and your middle. Create those fears, abilities and objects that will come in useful later. Hide a key, tell a secret, set an alarm, light a fire. Introduce a nosy neighbour, a forgetful teacher, an annoying sister, a temperamental dog.

OK, me hearties, get digging.

*In our case, treasure equals useful story details. Check out the section called "Let's Be Specific" on page 76 for more details on, well, details.

STORY PROMPT
TREASURE

Let's dig up some treasure, shall we?
Our character is bored on the beach – her mum is reading,
and her stepdad is asleep. Our character is digging in the sand
when – *clunk!* – her spade hits something hard. The girl keeps
digging, but more carefully now, slowly uncovering the buried
object. She reaches into the hole and removes a ...

A what? I don't know; this is your story. So what is it?
What does it do? How did it come to be buried in
the sand? How long has it been there? Is it alive?

You have 30 minutes to find out. Have fun!

EVEN MONSTERS NEED HELP SOMETIMES
CREATE YOUR OWN WRITER'S GROUP

Writing is harder than football, rugby, netball or hockey. Sure, you're unlikely to get kicked in the shins or hit over the head with a stick when you're writing a story (unless you have a very unusual method), but writing is something you do without the support of a team.

When you're stuck with a story problem – when your characters don't know what to do next, when you can't find the right way to describe something – it's just you and your Creative Monster. And that can be tough.

So why not create your own team? Find a friend who likes to write. Read each other's work, discuss your problems and your triumphs. Tell your friend when their writing is great, and help them find places where it could be better. Talk about what you're reading and what inspires you. Swap books, trade tips.

Better still, find a few people and form a writers' group.* You can meet once a week or once every fortnight. Whatever works best for you. At each meeting, somebody (if not everybody) should read something they have written since the last meeting. Then you can discuss it as a group. As well as getting some honest opinions about your stories, being part of a group encourages you to write something new in time for the next meeting.

*For some reason, writers' groups – of all sizes – tend to be called writers' circles. But what if you only have three? Surely that makes you a writers' triangle. And ten would be a writers' decagon? Now that I think about it, writers' circle is much simpler – let's stick with that.

GUIDELINES FOR A WRITERS' CIRCLE (OR HEXAGON, OR WHATEVER)

1. **Be considerate**. Remember how hard you work on your stories and assume your fellow writers have worked just as hard on theirs. Point out the good stuff before you point out any ways it might be improved.

2. **Learn to take criticism**. If someone points out a possible problem with your story, remember they are trying to help. And they might be right.

3. And they might be wrong. In which case, just **say thank you and smile**.

4. **It's not a competition**. You are there to have fun, help and encourage each other.

5. **Be honest**. You aren't helping anyone if you tell them a story is perfect, when in reality it needs fixing.

6. But being honest doesn't mean you can't **be gentle**.

7. When it's your turn to host, **always have biscuits**. Creative Monsters love biscuits.

FEEDING YOUR CREATIVE MONSTER

FINDING INSPIRATION

VITAMIN I

I LICKED THEM ALL FIRST, SO THEY SHOULD BE NICE AND EASY TO SWALLOW.

YOU'RE A GOOD FRIEND!

Ideas, as we know, come from your Creative Monster. Your monster searches them out, digs them up, chases them down and – when necessary – wrestles them to the ground.

It's hard work being a Creative Monster, and to do their job well they need to eat a full and varied diet rich in Vitamin I (you know, Inspiration). Good sources of Vitamin I include books, films, music, observations, conversations, questions and lemonade.

This next section will give you some tips on where to find plenty of fresh and juicy inspiration. So grab a basket and walk this way.

YOUR MONSTER'S FAVOURITE FOOD
BOOKS, BOOKS AND MORE BOOKS

Nothing makes a Creative Monster's mouth water like a good book. Fiction, non-fiction, serious, funny, scary – monsters are just crazy for pages. And the more you read, the bigger and stronger your Creative Monster grows.

Read the authors you love, and read authors you've never read before. If you're a girl, ask a boy to recommend something new. And if you're a boy, ask a girl. Read old books as well as new. Visit the library and pick up something that you normally wouldn't – who knows, you might love it. And even if you don't, your Creative Monster will gobble it up. So, read. A lot.

"READ A LOT. READ ANYTHING YOU CAN GET YOUR HANDS ON."
J.K. ROWLING

(I ASSUME YOU ARE FAMILIAR WITH THE WORK OF MS ROWLING?)

EXERCISE
READ SOMETHING

That's right, I want you to put this book down, then go and pick up another. Read for 30 minutes. And then go to your notebook and see if you can write down ideas or titles for five stories. Or more!

Maybe they will be based on the book you have been reading. Or perhaps they will be completely different. Whatever they are, I bet they will be wonderful.

BE NOSY

OBSERVE PEOPLE AND WATCH THE WORLD

All writers have a story radar inside their heads. Radars are devices used to detect large objects that are somehow hidden from sight, like sunken ships or high-flying aeroplanes. Your story radar detects ideas. And the more you use it, the stronger it gets.

Pay attention to your neighbours, watch people on the streets, listen to the way folk talk. Carry your notebook too, so you can jot down all the interesting things you see and hear. Sketch pictures. Ask people what they do and where they are from. Ask as many questions as you can. And listen carefully to the answers.

Take your Creative Monster for a stroll. Look around. Look up at the buildings, climb a tree, take in the view and walk a different way home. Read magazines and labels and instructions. Listen to music, listen to the news, listen to the weather, watch a documentary.

Collect unusual words and locations. Collect information. Collect people. You may not know what they are for immediately, but sooner or later these things will suggest a story, or a story will suggest these things.

Stand still while the world flows around you. Keep your eyes, your ears and your nostrils open. Be curious and inquisitive. And if anyone asks what you are doing up that tree, tell them: I am a writer, and I'm doing my job.

STORY PROMPT

A GHOST THAT IS AFRAID OF LIVING PEOPLE

Where is your story set? Where does this ghost exist – in a church, a graveyard, an abandoned house? Who is the ghost, and how did it become one? And who is the person or people that will disturb this ghost's peace? Can the people and the ghost communicate? And if so, how? Can the character help your ghost overcome its fears? And is there any way the ghost can help your characters?

STEAL SOMETHING

TAKE INSPIRATION FROM YOUR FAVOURITE AUTHORS

If you're stuck for a story idea, why not write a story inspired by one of your favourite books, TV shows or movies? I'm not suggesting you take the whole story idea and write it out in your own words – that would be a lot of hard work for little reward.* I'm suggesting you write a story based on existing characters, or set in their fictional world.

Write a story set in Hogwarts, Narnia or Middle Earth. Mix the characters up if you like. Create a story featuring Willy Wonka and Luke Skywalker. Paddington and Pooh Bear. Matilda and Mowgli. Oh, and let's not forget the Borrowers. You can borrow them too.

*The writer Hunter S. Thompson once copied out a novel by the legendary author Ernest Hemingway. He did this to try and understand how the great writer worked. It should be noted, however, that Hunter S. Thompson was famously crazy.

EXERCISE
HELP YOURSELF

I think you know what to do ... pick a book from your shelves, a film or a TV programme, and write a story set in that world or using those characters. And remember, you can mix the elements up if you want to. If you're not sure where to start, why not make yourself a character in the story?

Imagine it's your first day at Hogwarts, or that Paddington Bear moves into the house next door. Maybe your parents find an old wardrobe in a junk shop and bring it home, completely unaware that it leads to the land of Narnia? Perhaps the BFG peeps through your window at midnight...

MUUUUMMM!
I'M JUST POPPING TO THE MAGICAL LAND IN THE WARDROBE – DO YOU WANT ANYTHING?

THE MOST POWERFUL WORDS FOR WRITERS

WHAT IF?

Let me tell you the two most powerful words* known to writers the world over: **what if?**

You know: "What if cars could fly?"; "What if the world was ruled by apes?"; "What if I had a pet unicorn?"

Look at the world around you, listen to the things people say, think about the things you enjoy and those that you don't. Think about the stories you read and the films you watch. Then ask your Creative Monster: **what if?**

Think about football, dinosaurs, aliens, dance, sharks, monkeys, diamonds, giants, magic, mountains, aeroplanes and ships. And ask your Creative Monster: **what if?**

BEHOLD, THE SPHERE OF DESTINY.

THEY HAVE PAINTED THE VAST OUTDOOR CARPET WHITE IN PLACES.

HURRY UP! WE'LL BE EXTINCT BY THE TIME THIS KICKS OFF.

*The most powerful single word known to writers is "biscuits". Particularly those ones with chocolate on top.

Think about astronauts, teachers, scientists, inventors, pirates, soldiers, lawyers, doctors and dentists. And when you have, why not ask your Creative Monster: **what if?**

Think about foreign countries and cultures. Think about art. Think about food. Think about nature. Think about the past and the future. And, ask your Creative Monster, come on now, say it with me: **what if?**

Look at some aspect of the world, then change it. Add something, take something away, reinvent the rules. Take two things and combine them. Take three things and shake them all about. Just use your imagination and ask your Creative Monster: **what if?**

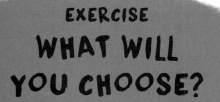

EXERCISE
WHAT WILL YOU CHOOSE?

Here's a whopping great list of "what ifs". Some I made up, some you might recognize from books you have read or films you have watched. Some have been used more than once. And they can all be used again.

What if you pick one now and write a story about it?

A WHOPPING GREAT LIST OF "WHAT IFS"

1. What if elephants could fly?

2. What if you were abducted by aliens?

3. What if there was a school especially for witches and wizards?

4. What if you found a suitcase full of money?

5. What if a blind man wanted to paint portraits?

6. What if you could travel through time?

7. What if your mum was the Prime Minister?

8. What if the Queen farted on live television?

9. What if gravity stopped working?

10. What if you could move objects with the power of your mind?

11. What if a magician lost his magic powers?

12. What if your brother was an evil genius?

13. What if dinosaurs were brought back to life?

14. What if a girl made friends with a giant? A friendly one.

15. What if a bear could talk?

A FEAR OF CLOWNS AND OTHER AVERSIONS
STARTING A STORY WITH A CHARACTER

Often, we begin a story by thinking up a great situation, quest, problem or "what if?" But we can also start a story with a character. Particularly if they have something called an aversion. An aversion is a strong dislike or fear of something. Here are a few examples:

- A fear of heights, dogs, spiders, ghosts, loud noises.
- A dread of public speaking, confined spaces, clowns.
- A loathing for opera music, mushrooms, football.

But how do we turn that into a story? That's right, we make our character face the thing they fear. We drop them into a situation guaranteed to make them squirm and suffer.

- The girl with a fear of clowns*: guess what's turning up at her friend's birthday party...
- The boy with a fear of heights: I suppose we'll have to get him up a tree somehow.
- The man who hates opera: what if he falls in love with ... an opera singer?

So let's build a character with an aversion, and then build a story around them, the way an oyster builds a perfect pearl around a grain of sand (they really do!)...

*A fear of clowns is a real thing and it's called coulrophobia.

152

LET'S MAKE SOMEONE SUFFER

Before you think of the aversion, let's build a realistic character with a name, a job and one or two traits (take a look at page 40–41 for inspiration) to make them interesting.

Then add an aversion.

Then think of the worst thing that could happen to that character.

And then make it happen. It's a wicked thing to do, but it makes wonderful stories.

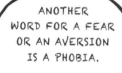

ANOTHER WORD FOR A FEAR OR AN AVERSION IS A PHOBIA.

I HAVE NO IDEA WHY, BUT SOME PEOPLE HAVE A PHOBIA OF MONSTERS! IT'S CALLED TERAPHOBIA.

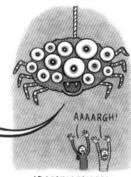

ARACHNOPHOBIA
(SPIDERS)

POGONOPHOBIA
(BEARDS)

SELENOPHOBIA
(THE MOON)

ZOOPHOBIA
(ANIMALS)

LEUKOPHOBIA
(THE COLOUR WHITE)

AEROPHOBIA
(FLYING)

CLAUSTROPHOBIA
(SMALL SPACES)

MAYBE IT'S A MOVIE, MAYBE IT'S A SONG
DIFFERENT WAYS TO TELL STORIES

There is more than one way to tell a story. We have books, of course, but there are also comics, cartoons, graphic novels, television, movies, theatre, audio books, poems, opera, ballet, nursery rhymes and songs. All of them tell stories, and all of them can be amazing.

So if you're having trouble writing a story, try telling it a different way.

- If your story contains tons of action, why not try it as a film or a cartoon?
- If it is very very short, see if you can turn it into a song.
- If it involves a lot of dialogue, it could work best as a play.

Any story can live in any format, and playing with these different options is huge fun.

EXERCISE
WRITE IT ANOTHER WAY

Remember earlier in the book when we were talking about avalanches? Well, now we're going to write about one. But I don't want you to write a traditional story. Write a song, or a poem. Draw a cartoon. Maybe you can create a dance inspired by the idea of an avalanche? Maybe you can write it as a film?

Films are written as **screenplays**. A screenplay is like a set of instructions to the people who will make the film. It describes what the audience will see. And what they will hear. What screenplays don't contain is the characters' thoughts. We have to show this information instead of telling it. The next page gives a short example of what a screenplay looks like.

Some of the terms may seem a little weird, but you don't need to worry about these right now. Just concentrate on the action and dialogue – that's pretty much all screenplays are. If you want to learn more, there are many good books and websites on how to write for film.

FILMS DON'T HAVE TO BE TWO HOURS LONG. THEY CAN BE AS SHORT AS ONE MINUTE, AND SOME VERY GOOD ONES ARE.

THE FIRST LINE TELLS US WHERE AND WHEN THE SCENE IS SET. "EXT." IS SHORT FOR EXTERIOR, IN OTHER WORDS THE SCENE IS SHOT OUTSIDE. IF IT'S INSIDE, WE USE "INT." FOR INTERIOR.

WHEN WE FIRST INTRODUCE CHARACTERS, WE USE CAPITALS.

EXAMPLE
SCREENPLAY

IMPORTANT IMAGES AND DETAILS (LIKE A CLOSE-UP SHOT OF BRYN'S FACE) ARE WRITTEN IN CAPITALS.

EXT. MOUNTAIN. DUSK.

Snow everywhere. We see THREE CLIMBERS (BRYN, PATRICK, HANK) — they look like tiny black dots on the vast landscape of pure glistening white. They trudge upwards.

CLOSE UP: BRYN'S FACE. He is exhausted. Snow in his beard and eyebrows. HIS EYES NARROW. He stops. Raises his hand in a signal for the other climbers to stop.

                    HANK
              What is it?

Bryn holds a gloved hand to his lips. SHH! His face is fixed in concentration. He listens and hears a LOW RUMBLE.

IMPORTANT SOUNDS ARE ALSO WRITTEN IN CAPITALS.

Patrick hears it too. He looks CONCERNED. He looks at Hank and Hank nods.

The distant rumble grows in volume until it sounds like booming THUNDER.

CUT TO:

THE SUMMIT. Snow beginning to slide down the mountain. WAVES AND WAVES OF SNOW.

                    BRYN
          Avalanche! Run!!!

They run.

DIALOGUE IS WRITTEN IN THE CENTRE OF THE PAGE UNDERNEATH THE SPEAKER'S NAME.

JEFF
I'M REALLY ENJOYING THIS BOOK. THERE'S A GOOD BIT ABOUT BUM GLUE COMING UP.

AVALANCHE! RUN!!!

GET REAL

INSPIRATION FROM YOUR OWN LIFE

Did something happen today that made you angry? Write it down. Write down the incident and capture exactly what that anger felt like.* You can use that later in your writing.

Did someone let you down? Write it down. Maybe you can use this as the start of a story. Did your brother steal your favourite jumper and get it covered in grass stains? Was a teacher mean? Was lunch disgusting? Write it down. Is something worrying you? Turn it into words and trap it on a page.

And don't forget the good stuff. The anticipation of a birthday, the excitement of Diwali, the taste of freshly baked cake. Write them down now and they're yours forever.

*An interesting side effect of doing this is that you often stop feeling angry. The thing that upset you can seem more understandable and less offensive when we turn it into words on a page. This goes equally well for fear, disappointment and, in some cases, toothache.

WRITE IT OUT TO WORK IT OUT

Think about a real-life experience you have had in the last few months. It can be something happy, surprising, worrying or annoying. Just so long as it created a strong feeling or emotion in you – joy, surprise, pain, disappointment, excitement. Or anything else.

And then write it down.

Write it exactly as it happened to you.

Or turn it into a piece of fiction.

Change the names of the characters if you like, play with the details, make it more or less dramatic. Add aliens. Add a ghost. Give it any ending you want.

But do try and capture the original emotion or feeling, because that emotion will give your writing power. Power you can unleash on some other story some other time.

BUM GLUE

HOW TO STAY PUT IN YOUR WRITING CHAIR

Inspiration can come at any time – when you're in bed, in the shower, bored at the back of class. But a place where it comes most often is at your desk, when you have made the decision to sit down and write.

However, one of the hardest things about writing is staying in your chair instead of wandering off and doing something else. That's because writing is challenging. (But that's also what makes it so rewarding.)

So how do we stay in our chair? Where do we find the discipline to stay put and get on with it? Easy. We use bum glue.

Now before you go running off to fetch your glue stick, stop! I don't mean real glue. It's a metaphor for anything that helps you stay on your chair for five minutes. My bum glue comes in three varieties:

BUM GLUE #1:
A SIGN FOR THE DOOR

That's right, I want you to design a sign. It might say something like:

When you stick this sign to your door, something interesting happens. The sign tells people that you are taking your writing seriously. And when you tell the world you mean business, your Creative Monster hears the message too.

That reminds me: you might want to put a picture of your Creative Monster on the sign. Like a security guard to send away unwelcome visitors.

BUM GLUE #2
MUSIC

I love writing to music, but it has to be the right kind of music. Nothing too distracting, otherwise I end up dancing when I should be writing. And nothing too mellow, otherwise I might fall asleep.

I have several "writing playlists", depending on the mood I want to create (energetic, sad, dramatic, happy). And how long I want to write for. I have one that's four hours long. And another that lasts for just 30 minutes.

But here's the trick: they all start with the same song.* So, whenever I hear that song, my Creative Monster knows it's time to get to work. (This can be a little confusing if I hear my writing song when I'm in a restaurant.)

I want you to put together your own writing playlist. Why not start with a four-song list that runs for about 15 minutes?

"AMATEURS SIT AND WAIT FOR INSPIRATION, THE REST OF US JUST GET UP AND GO TO WORK."

STEPHEN KING

(WORLD-FAMOUS WRITER OF SCARY STORIES AND FABULOUS TALES, AND ONE OF MY ALL-TIME FAVOURITE AUTHORS.)

MORNING!

*"Down by the River" by Neil Young. It's 9 minutes and 18 seconds long. Just enough to get me going.

BUM GLUE #3
A REWARD

I'm guessing this might be your favourite variety of bum glue. It's really simple. You say to yourself something like:

"I'm going to write for ten minutes, and when I'm finished, I'm going to have a glass of ice-cold lemonade."

"I'm going to write for 30 minutes. And when I finish, I'm going to watch some TV."

"I'm going to write for one whole hour. And when I'm done, I'm going to go for a bike ride."

What will your reward be?

MY REWARD IS DOING SOME DRAWING.

I GET TO DO A HUNDRED CARTWHEELS.

MY REWARD IS A NICE CUP OF TEA.

AND I TREAT MYSELF TO A TASTY BOOK.

STORY PROMPT
A STUCK BUM

I mean, come on! We're not letting this idea go to waste. Only this is no longer a metaphor, this is the real thing. Let's glue someone's butt to something.

So, questions:

➤ Whose butt? A teacher, a parent, a kid, a train driver, a policeman?

➤ What are they glued to? A seat, a bench, a tree, a fence, a wall, someone else?

➤ Who did the glueing? And why?

Answer the above questions and you have two things:

1. A very stuck, very angry person.

2. A story!

Go. Get sticking. Get writing.

HELP FROM ROOSTER AND MOUSE*
STORY PROMPTS, TITLES AND "WHAT IFS" FROM RUBY AND EVIE

1. **The Locked Room.** First things first, where is this room? In a hotel, at an eccentric relative's house, in school, at home? And who locked it? Why? What's inside? Where is the key, and what happens when your character finds it?

*My girls are probably going to be mad at me for embarrassing them by telling you their nicknames. But embarrassing your children is one of the benefits of being a parent. As I'm sure you already know.

2. Walking in the park, you see a sprawling oak tree surrounded by a fence – presumably to keep people out. But what if the fence is there to keep the tree in? Why would that be? Does the tree walk? Is it haunted? You tell us.

3. You find a four-leaf clover on a walk up a mountainside. They're said to be lucky. Is this one? If it is, how would the character's luck change? And then, what might happen if they lose the lucky clover?

4. **The Portal to Elsewhere** – what a great title! But where does this portal go? Where is this "elsewhere"? Underground, underwater, outer space? And what kind of portal is it – a doorway, a window in the air, a pit of quicksand? You tell me.

SEE YOU AGAIN LATER!

5. You walk past a shop window. In it stands a mannequin, dressed as if to go to a party. You notice mud on the mannequin's shoes, and then … the mannequin twitches. What happens next?

6. The Mystery of the Stolen Crown. Whose crown? A king, a queen? Or is it a prop from a play, or a toy, or part of a costume? And when is this set? In the present or the past? Or even the future? And who on earth took the crown? I guess that's the mystery.

7. Imagine a plague that doesn't give you boils, doesn't make you sick and won't kill you. It simply makes you fart. And it's very, very contagious.

8. What if you could see through someone else's eyes for a day? But whose eyes, and what will they show you?

9. The School for Robbers. This is a great idea, isn't it? A school where you learn to pick locks, climb drainpipes and run whilst carrying a sack of money. What other things would happen at a school like that? And wouldn't all your things get stolen?

10. The Shrinking Man. Poor man! Why is he shrinking? Think how frightening the world must become as you grow smaller. Dogs would appear as big as horses, horses as big as dinosaurs! What will happen when this man becomes so small that we can't even see him? Can it be stopped?

167

11. The Electric World. When I read this, I thought – but we already live in an electric world. TVs, music players, smartphones, computers, video games, electric cars, electric ovens, electric lights. And then I thought, what would happen if electricity ran out and we could no longer use all the electric devices we have come to rely on? That sounds like a good story to me.

12. A witch swaps the minds of a little girl and her pet cat. Think how fast you could run inside a cat's body, and how high you could jump! On the downside, the food is pretty awful, and you wouldn't be able to talk, only meow. And what would a cat do with your body? Where would it go? What would it eat? What would it say?

13. The Plastic Gobbler. I like this one; it feels like a story about the environment, and the Plastic Gobbler sounds like something that might help save the planet from plastic pollution. But what is it – maybe a machine, maybe a monster? It's up to you.

14. What if a policeman was secretly a bank robber? Was he always a criminal, and did he join the police so that he could get away with crimes? Or did he start off good and somehow turn bad? What could he get away with? And who will catch him?

15. **The End of Chocolate!** What a terrifying thought! But why has chocolate ended? Did we run out? Was it banned? Did we lose the recipe? What happens at Easter? What if someone discovers a small amount somewhere? It would be more valuable than gold!

PSSSST! WANNA BUY SOME CHOCOLATE?

MAYBE YOU CAN COMBINE TWO OF THESE IDEAS TO CREATE A BRAND-NEW PROMPT? FOR EXAMPLE, WHAT IF "THE PORTAL TO ELSEWHERE" FROM PROMPT 4 LED TO THE DISCOVERY OF "THE PLASTIC GOBBLER" FROM PROMPT 13? MIXING UP PROMPTS 10 AND 12 WOULD CAUSE QUITE AN INTERESTING SITUATION, AS WOULD MASHING UP NUMBER 7 AND NUMBER 9.

HOORAY!

Well done! You and your Creative Monster have put in a lot of work to reach the end of this book. So take a moment to pat yourself on the back and stroke your Creative Monster's fur. You've written many stories together, completed several exercises and considered lots of ideas for improving your writing.

CONGRATULATIONS
(AND A WORD ABOUT EGGS)

We've looked at goals and obstacles, similes and metaphors, showing and telling, arcs and Arks, tenses and senses, neologisms, dialogue, rhythm and a whole lot more. I hope this book has informed, entertained and inspired you. I hope it has made your Creative Monster roar like the magnificent beast it is.

But there's one more thing we need to discuss before we go any further. Rules. There are a lot of so-called "rules" for writing, but rules are like eggs. Not everyone likes them, some are bad and all of them were made to be broken. The ideas in this book are not rules. They are tools, tips and options.

And you should – like many brilliant writers before you – choose which ideas to use and which to ignore. It's important that you develop your own style. Otherwise, all our stories will end up sounding the same, and that would be rubbish.

I hereby give you permission to mix your metaphors, to create a hero without a goal, to place a gun on the mantelpiece and have nobody fire it. I want you to tell and not show. Ignore the senses and forget the specifics. Write a story that ends: "it was all a dream."

After all, we have a Creative Monster on our team, and monsters – let me tell you – they do whatever the heck they want. Whatever feels good, exciting and – most importantly – fun.

Because when you're having fun, it shows in your writing, making it fizz and crackle and burst into life. When you have fun writing a story, the people reading it will have fun too.

So trust in your Creative Monster, let your imagination run free, your stories run wild, and your pencil fly across the page. Write confident, write crazy, write dangerous. Write your way. Because you are the only one who can.

Go, get to it. Write something wonderful!

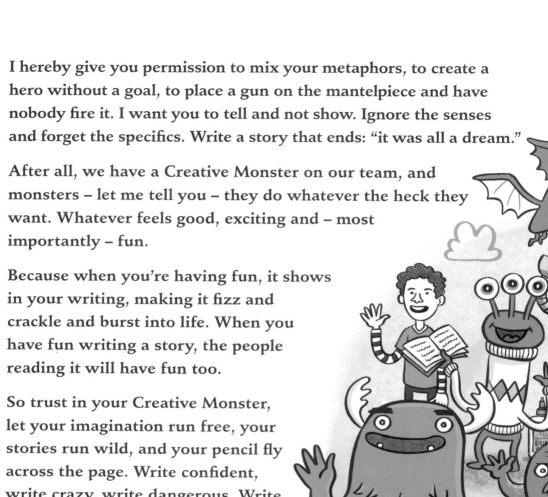

Can you find: 6 dinosaur eggs, 5 aliens, 4 bottles of bum glue, 3 snails, 2 frogs and 1 golden banana?

INDEX

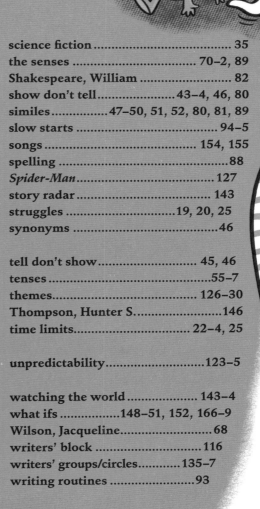